**SARAH M. ZERWIN**

Foreword by Cris Tovani

# STEP ASIDE

## Strategies for Student-Driven Learning with Secondary Readers and Writers

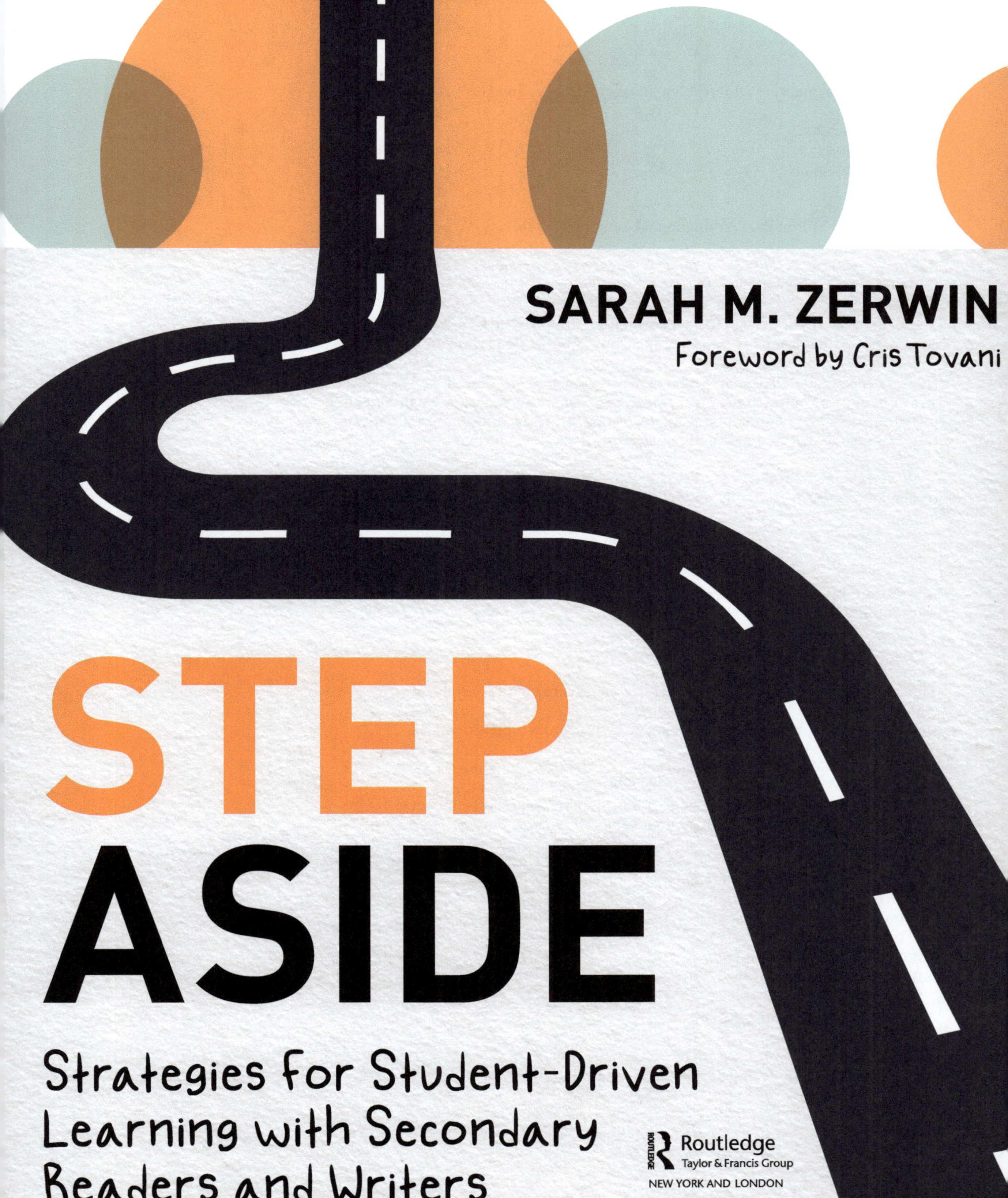
SARAH M. ZERWIN
Foreword by Cris Tovani
STEP
ASIDE
Strategies for Student-Driven
Learning with Secondary
Readers and Writers
Routledge
Taylor & Francis Group
NEW YORK AND LONDON
A Stenhouse Book

Designed cover image: © Dmytro Synelnychenko/Getty Images

First published 2025
by Routledge
605 Third Avenue, New York, NY 10158

and by Routledge
4 Park Square, Milton Park, Abingdon, Oxon, OX14 4RN

*Routledge is an imprint of the Taylor & Francis Group, an informa business*


*Credits:*

Illustrations by JaneMelyn Zerwin Strode
Author photo by Courtney Nicholson-Paine

*Library of Congress Cataloging-in-Publication Data*
Names: Zerwin, Sarah M., author.
Title: Step aside : strategies for student-driven learning with secondary readers and writers / Sarah M. Zerwin.
Description: New York, NY: Routledge, 2025. | Includes bibliographical references and index. |
Identifiers: LCCN 2024027935 (print) | LCCN 2024027936 (ebook) | ISBN 9781625316554 (paperback) | ISBN 9781032682488 (ebook)
Subjects: LCSH: Student-centered learning. | Language arts (Secondary) | Language arts–Correlation with content subjects. | Classroom management.
Classification: LCC LB1027.23 .Z426 2025 (print) | LCC LB1027.23 (ebook) | DDC 371.39/4–dc23/eng/20240904
LC record available at https://lccn.loc.gov/2024027935
LC ebook record available at https://lccn.loc.gov/2024027936

ISBN: 9781625316554 (pbk)
ISBN: 9781032682488 (ebk)

DOI: 10.4324/9781032682488

Typeset in Adobe Text Pro
by Deanta Global Publishing Services, Chennai, India

# Dedication

To Mom

# Contents


**Foreword by Cris Tovani** xiii

**Acknowledgments** xvii

**Chapter 1** **Introduction** 1

Stepping Aside to Center Students 4

Teaching Students *How* to Drive the Work of Reading, Writing, and Thinking 8

Cultivating Student Agency Above All Else 11

**Chapter 2** **Invite Students to Drive as Readers** 13

How Can We Invite Students to Drive as Readers? 16

*Start Small*: Teach Students to Use Original Thought Annotations to Capture Their Initial Ideas Based on the Small Things They Notice 20

*Seek Connections*: Teach Students to Connect Their Ideas to Grow Their Thinking 24

- Rambling Thoughts 24
- Concept Mapping 27
- Other Step Two Strategies 28
  - Two-Page Spreads 32

Small-Group Shared Work 32
Conversation 32
*Take Action*: Tasks for Step Three in the Meaning Making Process 33
A Quick Word About (Not) Grading and Assessment 33
The Goal Is Independence 38

**Chapter 3 Invite Students to Drive as Writers** 41
How Can We Invite Students to Drive as Writers? 42
Model Writing Process by Driving Alongside Writers 44
*Start Small*: Teach Students to Capture Their Initial Thinking About Their Writing 45
Invite Students to Answer the Magic Question 45
Invite Frequent, Small Revision Tasks 47
*Seek Connections*: Teach Students to Get Ideas to Strengthen Their Writing 49
Using Mentor Texts: An Independent Strategy for Students to Strengthen Their Writing 51
Finding Mentor Texts 51
Studying Mentor Texts 53
Finding Just-Right Readers for Feedback: A Strategy for Students to Work with Others to Strengthen Their Writing 55
Coach Students on How to Find the Just-Right Reader for a Particular Piece of Writing 55

Teach Students How to Give Their Readers Guidance as They Read 57

*Take Action*: Coach Students to Decide How They Want to Finalize Their Writing 58

Cleaning Up Mechanics 59

Polishing a Piece of Writing 60

A Quick Word About (Not) Grading and Assessment 63

The Goal Is Independence 64

**Chapter 4** **Invite Students to Drive the Conversation in the Classroom** 67

How Can We Invite Students to Drive Talk in the Classroom? 69

Teach Students to Talk with Each Other to Determine Meaning from a Shared Text 71

Teach Students to Talk with Each Other About Their Writing 74

Modeling Writing Conversations Between Two Writers 75

Whole-Class Workshopping a Single Piece of Writing 77

Teach Students to Talk with Each Other to Reflect on the Day-to-Day Work of the Classroom 79

A Quick Word About (Not) Grading and Assessment 81

The Goal Is Independence 82

Chapter 5 **Invite Students to Drive Assessment and Grading** 85

Teach Students How to Set Their Own Goals for Learning 87

- A Clear Set of Learning Goals 87
- Clearly Articulate Learning Progressions for Each of the Learning Goals 88
- Clearly Articulate the Learning Behaviors that Support the Learning Goals 91
- Invite Students to Make a Plan for Their Own Learning Journeys 93

Teach Students Strategies for Ongoing Reflection 97

Teach Students How to Evaluate Their Own Work 99

Hold Students Accountable for the Doing of the Work 100

- Help Students See How Fully and Completely They Are Doing the Work 101
- What to Put in the Score Boxes in the Gradebook 101
- Use Descriptive Rubrics to Show Students Clearly What Complete Work Means 102
- Invite Students to Help You Keep Track of Whether They're Doing the Work or Not 105

Help Students *See* Their Own Progress Toward Their Learning Goals 107
Provide Clear Guidelines for Final Grade Selection 109
The Most Valuable Part of the Process: The Final Grade Letter/Story 112
The Goal Is Independence 114

**Chapter 6** **Design the Classroom Space to Support Student-Driven Learning** 117
Scheduling Time Behind the Wheel with a Predictable Weekly Routine 119
- An Example Weekly Routine for a Writing-Centered Class 122
- An Example Weekly Routine for a Reading-Centered Class 126
- Remind Students How the Weekly Routine Centers *Their* Work 128

Helping Students Feel Safe in the Classroom Space 130
- Classroom Procedures and Policies 130
- Seating Charts 132
- Community Building 133

Co-Create Classroom Time and Space 135
The Goal Is Independence 137

**Chapter 7** **Student-Driven Learning Makes *Our* Work More Sustainable** 139
Student-Driven Learning Saves Us Time Planning and Preparing for Class 140
Student-Driven Learning Saves Us Time Responding to Students' Work 142

Student-Driven Learning Saves Us Time on Data Management 144
When Students Are Driving, They Do More While We Do Less 148

**Bibliography** 149
**Index** 155

# Foreword

Cris Tovani

**"What's the Purpose of School, Anyway?"**
—Jakai, seventh grader

Last spring, when Jakai asked me what the purpose of school was, it caught me off guard. I said something like, "Well, it's to get smarter about the world around you so you can have a happier life."

The response didn't seem to satisfy him because his next question was even more pointed, "How does filling in blanks about which dogs die in the book help me do that?"

Jakai's language arts class was listening to the teacher play aloud *The Call of the Wild*. Periodically, she would pause the recording and direct kids to open their laptops and find the slide she was projecting on the interactive whiteboard. She would then call out to students to see if anyone had the answer. When no one responded, she filled in the blank so kids could type the "right answer" into their electronic worksheet.

Jakai's teacher was using a district-prescribed curriculum. She wasn't deviating from it because she had been told to follow it. It was irrelevant that some kids weren't interested in the novel, or that it was too hard for many to read on their own. What mattered was that students followed directions so the teacher could check the lesson off of a prescribed scope and sequence that didn't seem to take learners into account.

Later that day, I heard Jakai's teacher in the main office lamenting, "These kids won't do a thing unless I tell them exactly what to do. They aren't invested and won't do the work without me being on them all the time." She was right. Her students didn't care about the curriculum, and she did have to stay "on them all the time," so that boredom-induced chaos didn't erupt. It seemed both the teacher and the students had given up their agency for teaching and learning.

Frankly, I don't think the fault lies in the students or the teachers. Schools have tested, ranked, and sorted learners right out of their agency. The fear of low test scores has pushed some districts to mandate "teacher proofed" curricula that demands fidelity to programs over fidelity to kids. It's no wonder students misbehave, play the game of school, or sit compliantly waiting for their teachers to tell them what to do.

A lot is riding on how educators deal with the lack of learner agency. Do we follow a curriculum that dictates our every move, or do we use curriculum as a resource that we adapt to meet the needs of students? Do we look to cognitive science to inform what students need in order to grow as readers, writers, and thinkers or do we trust people outside of the classroom to dictate how to keep students busy?

Deep down, we know that if we want students to get better at reading, writing, and thinking, we have to actually engage them in the process. Filling in electronic worksheets may keep kids occupied, but it's not going to radically improve their reading, writing, and critical thinking abilities. Teachers need to have agency as well. And that agency comes in the form of teachers adapting instruction so that students have opportunities to take the lead in their own learning.

Thank goodness there is a book to lead the way. Not one to shy away from challenging problems of practice, author Sarah Zerwin addresses head-on student and teacher agency. In her first book, *Point-Less,* Sarah helped readers consider grading in a way that puts learners at the center of the process. In this second book, Sarah provides new ideas on how to rebuild agency and ownership in both teachers and students.

Privileging process and growth over compliance and product, Sarah shows teachers how to put students in the driver's seat when it comes to learning. Three core beliefs drive her instruction: Trust learners to do important work, provide choice, and give students frameworks upon which to reflect and act. While reading *Step Aside,* I can almost hear Sarah whispering, "Trust students to think. Provide options in how they read, write, and discuss. And last, give them a framework to hold their thinking. With practice students will take ownership of their learning."

Choice drives engagement. Sarah teaches educators how to weave choice in with instruction. I'm not talking "a phone book-sized menu of choices" with so many options that it paralyzes users. I'm talking about managed choice, structured around elegantly simple frameworks.

These frameworks provide structure so that teachers can let go, giving students optimal ownership in how they engage in thinking about their reading, writing, and discussing. One of my favorite frameworks described in the book is the *Original Thought Annotations* or OTAs. Using OTAs, readers and writers can safely explore and take risks in how they think about, share, and use their literacy skills to learn about the world around them.

Sarah's ideas, student examples, and helpful checklists provide options that help teachers to step aside and let kids be the drivers of their learning. Readers will notice throughout the book how Sarah's students evolve from compliant learners to reflective thinkers.

Often I break an unspoken English teacher rule and read the last chapter way before I get to it. Reading ahead prepares me for the death of a beloved character or gives me comfort that the book is worthy of my time. I started at the last chapter of *Step Aside*—and I'm glad I did. Sarah gives readers not only permission to take something off their plates so students have time to take ownership of their learning, but she also encourages us to silence the phantom teacher on our shoulder telling us to do as we're told instead of what's best for learners.

As the title suggests, we need to step aside and let students in on the messiness of learning. We need to remove ourselves as obstacles as the keepers of knowledge and the puppeteers of student thinking and focus on process and improvement over product and mastery. So instead of tethering ourselves to prescribed programs, we need to focus on teaching students the behaviors of skillful readers, writers, conversationalists, and thinkers. Our very democracy depends on it. Imagine how much more sustainable our instruction could be if students had the agency to drive their own learning and their teachers had the confidence to step aside and let them.

# Acknowledgments

## BABY, THE

IYKYK. Since August of 2006, teaching alongside the folks in the language arts department at Fairview High School has kept me engaged in the important work we do together. My gratitude grows every year. Thank you for putting up with me. For indulging my ideas. For pushing back. For keeping me laughing. For listening. For the biting social commentary. For the book recommendations. For your masterful classroom moves. I'm always learning.

## CRUMPLED-UP PAPER IN MY MAILBOX AT SCHOOL

I know this is how my brother shows he's been thinking about me. John, I wouldn't have wanted to have anyone else by my side since 1973.

## DANCING IN THE KITCHEN WHILE WE MAKE DINNER

So maybe we didn't keep up with what newly dating us said we'd do every day forever. But I wouldn't trade the dance we've been on together. It's the daily who-can-get-home-to-walk-the-dog-after-school dance, and it's the ongoing dance of being who we are together—twenty-six years and counting. Paul, I'm grateful you still like me after all this time. I love you.

## DEMENTIA

Mom, you're fading. I love you. Very much. Thank you for showing me the value in deciding things for myself. (See also ENGINEERS.)

## ENCYCLOPEDIA OF AN ORDINARY LIFE

Inspiration for these alphabetized acknowledgments. (See also YOU for a shameless theft of how Amy Krause Rosenthal ended her clever and inspirational memoir.)

## ENGINEERS

Key object of my earliest lesson about agency. Courtesy of my mom, Verna Su Holland Zerwin. (See also the end of Chapter 1.)

## FINGER IN THE WOUND

Sam, you did not only stick your finger in the wound. You wiggled it around. Ouch. But you were right—my sophomores did not know why they were doing the things. Thank you. (See also the start of Chapter 1.)

## FOREWORD 2.0

Cris, may I never write another book without a foreword by you.

## GREENERY

Courtney, thank you for scoping out the perfect backdrop and for saying we looked great as you snapped away. We're both introverts and awkward in photo sessions, but you kept us smiling. (See also back cover, photo here of author and illustrator, and CNP Photos online at www.thewildernessgems.com.)

## HEAD SPACE

Maddie (Student Teacher Extraordinaire), you were so ready to drive things for our sophomores that it freed up space in my thinking to finish this book. I'm grateful. And excited for you and your lucky future students and colleagues.

## "I COULD DO THAT SO MUCH BETTER."

That's what I was hoping you'd say, Jane, when I showed you my sketch of a possible comic feature for this book. I've treasured every moment we've spent side by side brainstorming ideas and looking over your drawings. Proud Mom over here. I love you!

## KAREN'S CHOCOLATE CHIP COOKIES

When I stepped away from Colorado Writing Project work to finish this book, I appreciated your support, Karen, more than you'll know. Thank you also to Sheila and Crystal and the rest of the folks I missed out on working with over the last many months. I hope you all enjoyed some cookies for me.

## KNOWING SO MANY OF THE SAME PEOPLE

Terry, I'm still amazed that we had never met each other until we started talking about this book. Your care for me and your enthusiasm for my work are exactly what I needed to keep writing. Thank you.

## KNOWLEDGE COMMUNITY, THE

So says the front of a composition notebook I found hidden away on my bookcase at school. Jay, it was the notebook we started many years ago to record the ever-swirling ideas that became the foundation of The Paper Graders. Those ideas kept swirling into this book, even though now you are highly recommending the life of a retired teacher. You're definitely doing it right. I'll get there. Eventually. (See also jaystottmusic.com.)

## LEG WARMERS

Making it possible for me to continue typing out this page in a chilly air-conditioned Brewing Market Cafe on the first day of June 2024. I wonder how many of the words of this book were written here?

## LEGO BUILDING VIDEOS ON YOUTUBE

You promised you would still get your work done if I put on that time-lapse video of the person building the huge Lego city. And then we were all mesmerized. Friday energy is like that. Thank you, students, for all of it—the words you wrote, the ideas you shared, the YOUs you brought into our classroom each day. Thank you, especially, for the insight you offered about my constant pedagogical experiments. Let's keep building our classroom together.

## MANTRA

"What would Katie Wood Ray do to make this sentence not have so many words?"

## NCTE 2022 and 2023

An opportunity to be in the same physical space with smart-as-hell new teacher friends I met on Twitter and got to know on Zoom during the dark hours of the pandemic: Jessyca, Joel, LaMar, Scott—thank you.

## OCTOPUSES

Now that this book is finished, I can do some writing to figure out my current obsession. Is it their flexibility? Their ability to multitask? Their unique personalities?

## ORANGE RUNWELLS

Thank you for the continued support and opportunities, Penny.

## PARKER PALMER

Reading a few pages in *The Courage to Teach* is how I started many writing sessions for this book. Somehow his words were always exactly what I needed to read.

## RADISHES

Soft English butter. Flaky Maldon salt. Cool radishes. Simple ingredients that come together for an unexpected powerhouse.

Space to be together. Dedicated time. Cool Radishes. A most unexpected powerhouse in my life. You lovely humans make me want to be a force for good in the universe.

## SANTA FE

Blue sky beyond my laptop screen. Hikes. Piñon. Quiet. Thank you, Amy and Harley, for letting me sit on the deck and write.

## SIGNED RELEASE FORMS

Alex, Allie, Emily, Isabel, Jake, Kai, Lucia, Oscar, Robin, Suriya, and Zach—you make the strategies in this book come alive. Thank you for letting me include your work, so readers don't just have to take my word for it.

## SLIDE DECKS

Conference presentations, consulting gigs, on-line workshops, school visits, Zoom drop-ins to book clubs reading *Point-Less*—each helped me to wrangle a bit more clarity to the ideas that ended up in this book. I am grateful for each invitation.

## SNEAKERS

My current preferred style of professional footwear. I can't quite pull it off with as much style as you though, Nawal. I'm grateful for text conversations at critical moments in the journey that this book has traveled.

## SQUISHMELLOWS

Though they're threatening to take over the office couch, I swear, they just jump into my shopping cart at King Soopers. Claire-Maria, Jaime, and Paul—our office is the heart of my existence at school. And it's not about the plushies. I'm a better teacher (and human) because of the constant conversation with you.

## THREE HOURS

Would repeated three-hour Sunday morning writing sessions finish a book while in the midst of teaching high school language arts with two new preps on my schedule? Not entirely. But we're here now. Barely.

## VISION

Tobey, you saw what this book could be before I was able to. Thank you.

## WAFFLES

See Chapter 6.

## YOU

Thank you for reading this book.

**Image A.1** About the illustrator: JaneMelyn Zerwin Strode is currently pursuing a bachelor of fine arts in drawing and painting at the University of Colorado at Boulder. You can see more of her art on Instagram @ janemelyn_

**Image A.2** JaneMelyn Zerwin Strode, *today I will lay on the ground and stew in this misery*, 2024, oil on canvas, 55 × 76 cm.

CHAPTER 1

# INTRODUCTION

“Wait, Doc Z, what if we made a podcast?”

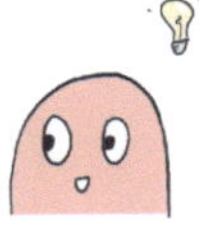

This. This is the energy I’m always hoping for.

Prior to this moment near the end of the fall semester, my sophomores had spent too many weeks on *Antigone*, with me making too many of the decisions about how they would engage with the text and about how they would write in response to it. So I was trying a few weeks anchored on more student choice—about what they read and about how they wrote in response to it. Hence the podcast question. There were two primary reasons for my change of approach.

One: I was exhausted due to the planning and prep work I had set for myself. We were reading one section of the play each week while watching a related bit of a film adaptation (*Antigone*, 2019 directed by Sophie Dersape). I tasked myself with figuring out a weekly reading focus along with selecting specific sections of the film to watch and then figuring how to help students find connections between the two—all while trying to come up with a piece of writing they might do that would engage them meaningfully and help them build their thinking. And then I had to do it all again the next week. For six weeks (because I had sectioned the play off into six chunks). It was a huge mental load. One that I had created for myself.

Two: Though I intended for my sophomores' weekly writing invitations to be meaningful, I had the feeling they were kind of phoning it in. They just weren't totally there, voices present. Not on the computer screens where they wrote. Not in their writer's notebooks where they dutifully showed me their reading response work—too structured by me—so I could stamp it off. (With an adorable dinosaur stamp that somehow made me feel like I wasn't enforcing blatant compliance.) Not in the stilted whole-class conversations I made space for each week that simply weren't working. It became obvious that little of it mattered that much to them. I felt like they were doing things only because I asked them to and because there was a grade at stake.

Sigh.

If you know anything about me as a teacher, you know that this vision of a classroom is far from what I intend. I aspire to a space where students are out front, driving the work. I even wrote an entire book about anchoring course grades on learning goals that students set *for themselves*! But here I was, spending way too much time planning weekly activities that weren't meaningful or even that engaging. Here I was, running a classroom where my students watched *me* do the thinking. How had I gotten so far off track?

I was trying to implement units based on bundles of standards created by my district—instructional goals that actually didn't work very well together.

I was trying to teach a course that aligned with what my colleagues were doing, so all our sophomores would have a similar learning experience—a value shared widely across my school and department.

I was trying to support my students. Their struggles as readers and writers seemed intensified following the disruptions caused by the pandemic.

And, as always, I was contending with the huge set of perceived expectations about what a language arts class is supposed to be. There's even a name for this: phantom policy (Franzak, 2008)—a concept that helped me unpack a similar moment in my instructional journey many years ago where I found myself standing in a darkened classroom essentially alone at an overhead projector. My students were completely zoned out and possibly sleeping all around me as I attempted to get them to help me fill out a table. Each row had *my* big question to consider for each chapter of *The Great Gatsby* and then space to record the major plot events that happened.

But I was the only one coming up with any ideas. I was Ferris Bueller's teacher working a room of basically catatonic students, droning on and on, asking, "anyone? anyone?" I answered all of my own questions and filled out the table all by myself. Something about the darkness, the painful silence, the overhead projector illuminating only me and *my* thinking made me consider how far I had strayed from my intentions.

At that painful moment of realization, I was in the middle of my dissertation research for graduate school. I only tell you this so you'll understand how carefully I had designed my intended instructional approach. I had spent at least two semesters intensely focused on methods to engage students with literature authentically, as humans who turn to books to help them make sense of their own lives, to put my students' responses to books at the center of our classroom, and to ultimately cede all powers of meaning making to them.

But there I was, having my own reading experience in front of them, totally silencing their voices and ideas, completely obscuring any opportunities to make meaning on their own. I'll spare you the heavy academic theorizing my dissertation had me unpacking at that moment, but it has to do with the phantom policy whispering in my ear about how I'm *supposed* to do things. It was as if there was some phantom English teacher, telling me what to do all the time, undercutting my confidence. You might have one, too. Maybe your phantom teacher looks like one of your past English teachers in college or high school. Maybe yours looks like the image the world seems to project of the belabored English teacher (reading glasses, cardigan sweater, sensible shoes?... wait, that *is* me on some days!). Mine whispers things to me like, "they need to read the classics," or "they won't be ready for college if they aren't writing formal academic essays," or "they won't take the work seriously if there's not a big grade on it" (yes, even though I wrote that book about not doing this).

No, phantom English teacher, what my students really need to do is read texts that matter to them, talk with each other about those texts, and use those conversations to help them figure out what they want to say as writers. On repeat.

In Franzak's study, "phantom policy" refers to the implicit expectations that teachers unknowingly carry in their heads that guide their decision making. It's whatever it is that makes teachers across the nation think every ninth-grade language arts course requires *Romeo and Juliet* and *The Odyssey*. Our phantom English teachers influence more than what texts it seems we are *supposed* to teach: they whisper to us about what and how our students should write, about how we should grade, about how we should run class, about how we should plan for our classrooms, about how we should interact with our students. Even twenty-eight years into my teaching career, my phantom English teacher still impacts the way I think about my classroom.

But we can talk back! When we stay in awareness about those moments when our phantom English teachers are trying to drive once again, we're presented with a powerful opportunity to reflect.

For example, though it was painful to recognize how far I had gotten off track of my instructional intentions while teaching *Antigone*, I remembered that my sophomores have their own ideas about what's worth reading, talking about, and writing about. Yes, a text like *Antigone* can absolutely be something they consider meaningful, but not in the way I was going about it. I was inviting compliance. And they were complying. And I'm pretty sure I was working much harder than they were.

With that reflection, I wrapped up *Antigone* as quickly as I could and instead spent the next few weeks simply reading texts that mattered to them, talking about those texts, and writing in response—however they wanted to respond. That's when some students wondered about producing a podcast for a weekly writing task. They were excited about their work. They were writing about topics I never would have put in front of them on my own. They were leading energetic conversations—the kinds where I had to work hard to keep up with the ideas bouncing around the room, student to student. As I reflected on the voice of my phantom English teacher, I once again remembered the importance of stepping aside to get out of my students' way so they could do work that actually mattered to them.

## Stepping Aside to Center Students

Stepping aside does not mean *actually* stepping aside—like completely out of the room and in the hall while the students do whatever they want in the classroom. It means that you curate an experience carefully and teach students strategic tools that they can use on their own in that curated space and beyond. When we notice our students struggling, especially, our phantom English teacher may nudge us to step in with too much scaffolding, too many directives, making too many of the decisions for them about their work. We do this with all the best intentions in the world because we want our students to find success. But we have to check ourselves and look instead for opportunities to teach them how to do the work on their own.

I offer a metaphor to think about this. When teaching teenagers how to drive, we don't just throw them the keys and a credit card and tell them to have fun. We teach them the rules of the road, how to operate the car, how to keep themselves—and others—safe while driving around. With that metaphor on the table, I want to take you back in time to young Sarah, learning how to drive.

I'm 15. Sophomore year. I've signed up for driver's ed, and I can't wait to start driving. Wheels equal freedom. The option to do what I want, when I want to, without having to get someone else to drive me around. In the suburban area of Denver where I spent my high school years, this was a big deal. The public bus wasn't practical, and everything was too far apart to walk to. My parents worked a decent commute away, so if I didn't want to take the school bus (and I didn't), I had to persuade friends to drive me around.

The terrible late 1980s-era, graphic, driver's ed videos are still etched in my memory... but not nearly as indelibly as the one day we got to actually *practice* driving. We got on a school bus and headed over to the district driving course located outside of the next high school over. It was a fenced-in asphalt expanse, with lines making up lanes, roads, intersections, and parking spaces with orange cones everywhere to mark things off. In pairs, we filled the handful of automatic transmission cars parked there and waiting for us. In the center of the asphalt sat a control booth, a small square building with windows on all sides, where our teacher sat and barked feedback at us over the AM frequency our radios were tuned into. "Slow down on the curve!" "Make sure you come to a complete stop!" "Five more minutes before you need to return the cars to where they were parked to begin with!"

In the little family four-door my friend Kathy and I had been assigned, we drove around, following the lane lines, avoiding the cones, laughing about the teacher's voice on the radio, wishing more than anything that we had more time behind the wheel.

Think about teenage you—remember how dearly you wanted as much time as possible behind the wheel? Not necessarily the literal car wheel, but in making your own choices about how you spent your time, what you focused on, what classes you could take, who you hung out with. Wanting to drive one's own existence is a key piece of adolescence.

This metaphor about teaching students how to literally drive is helpful in thinking about how we might approach classroom instruction in a way that helps us consider our role and identity as teachers while keeping us from doing the work *for* our students—the work that is most critical for them to be fully in control of. As you look over the driving course diagram shown in Figure 1.1, consider how the different locations on it represent different roles we can play for our students as they learn to drive the reading, writing, and thinking work of our classrooms. Thinking about who you are as a teacher, where do you see yourself? Which of these stances apply to you? Which one seems to be the primary way you think about your role as a teacher?

The truth is that you probably take all of the stances described in Figure 1.1—each is certainly necessary at different times. But taking them singularly without tempering them with the other stances can create a classroom space not so conducive to learning.

For example, we have to be in the control tower (stance 1) when we post final course grades. Our students can't do that on their own. But we can minimize the impact of the looming final grade by designing a different path to that grade that students can drive essentially themselves.

Teenagers are funny. If we don't take time to laugh and play with them (stance 2), we lose an important opportunity for community building. But if this is *all* we do in the classroom together, very little actual learning would get done.

Helping students feel connected to each other, to the classroom, and to the teacher goes a long way toward heading off conflict (stance 3). But if our classrooms don't also welcome the tension created by students who might disagree with each other (and the teacher!), then some critical learning opportunities are lost.

People need meaningful invitations to embark on work. They need deadlines to bring work to completion (stance 4). But there are plenty of unique circumstances for individual students that impact their time and the pace at which they work. Our classrooms can also be flexible to account for those unique needs.

And, of course it's important for us to hang out on the edge of our classrooms sometimes (stance 6) and quietly observe what is happening.

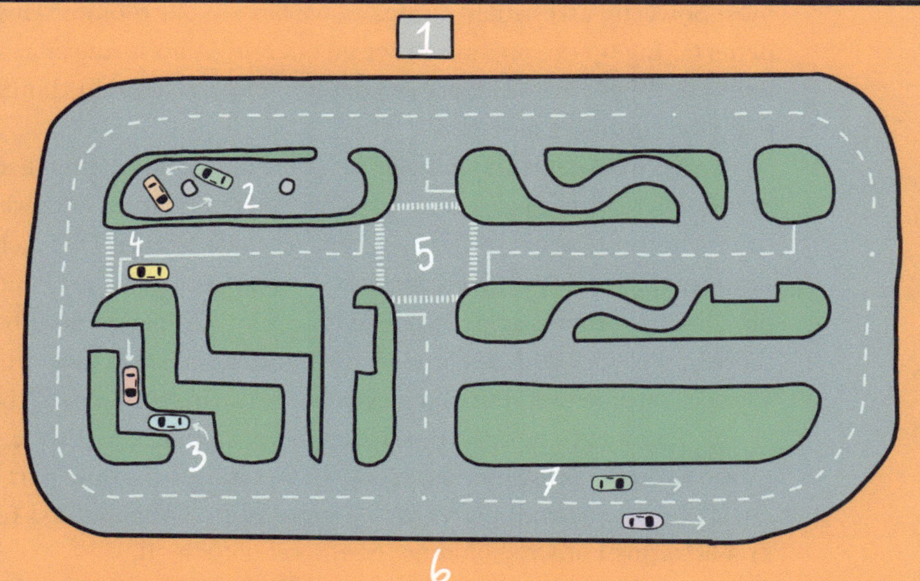


## WHERE ARE YOU?

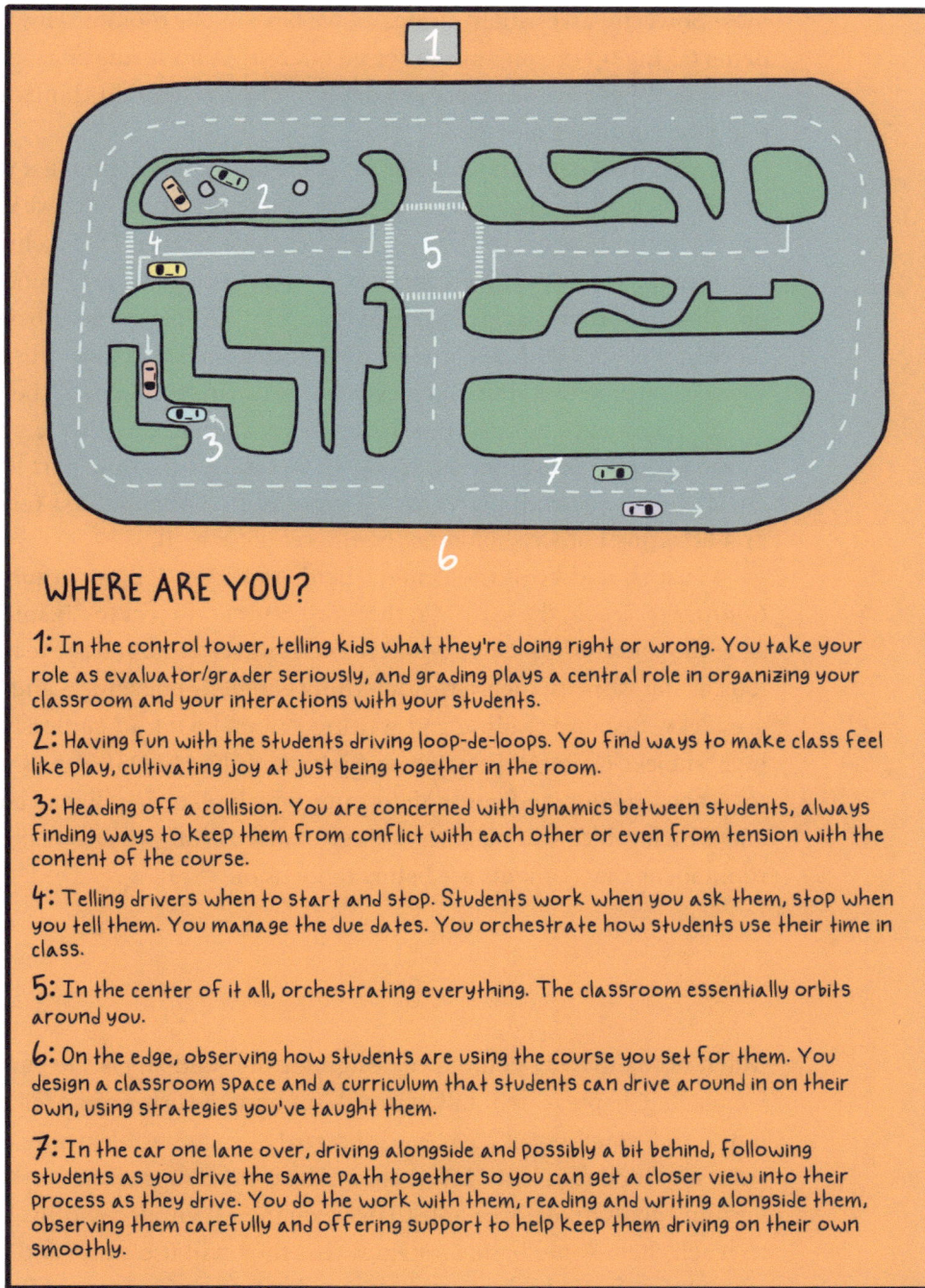

**1:** In the control tower, telling kids what they're doing right or wrong. You take your role as evaluator/grader seriously, and grading plays a central role in organizing your classroom and your interactions with your students.

**2:** Having fun with the students driving loop-de-loops. You find ways to make class feel like play, cultivating joy at just being together in the room.

**3:** Heading off a collision. You are concerned with dynamics between students, always finding ways to keep them from conflict with each other or even from tension with the content of the course.

**4:** Telling drivers when to start and stop. Students work when you ask them, stop when you tell them. You manage the due dates. You orchestrate how students use their time in class.

**5:** In the center of it all, orchestrating everything. The classroom essentially orbits around you.

**6:** On the edge, observing how students are using the course you set for them. You design a classroom space and a curriculum that students can drive around in on their own, using strategies you've taught them.

**7:** In the car one lane over, driving alongside and possibly a bit behind, following students as you drive the same path together so you can get a closer view into their process as they drive. You do the work with them, reading and writing alongside them, observing them carefully and offering support to help keep them driving on their own smoothly.

**Figure 1.1** Driving Course
Where are you during a typical instructional experience?

This is similar to Owocki and Goodman's kidwatching (2002)—one of the most powerful assessment strategies we have in our toolbox. How are students taking up the invitations we've offered? Who seems engaged? Who doesn't? Where are students getting hung up? Where do things seem to really be humming along? Why?

There are aspects about the *process* of reading and writing that we teach better when we're engaged in the work ourselves, too. So there's a bit of driving the course ourselves that we need to do (stance 7). Teaching from *inside* of the reading and writing of our classrooms gives us a vantage point on what the process steps look like that is impossible without being right there in the work with our students. We may not be able to do this fully for every classroom task, but doing even part of an assignment can help.

You may have noticed that I skipped over stance 5. This is because I caution you in taking on this stance. In fact, this is the only part I actually *don't* think we should play. Our classrooms are not about *us*. Yes, we are orchestrating but we should not be the center of it all.

What should be at the center, then? As Parker Palmer argues in *The Courage to Teach*, the learning, the work, a great subject to dig into should sit at the center of our classrooms. Something students and the teacher can look at and work on together. Something endlessly engaging—and here we are lucky, because reading and writing can make for an endlessly engaging, "subject-centered" classroom (Palmer, 2017, 117–23). When we work together *with* our students to determine which texts they'll read and write and which topics will be at the center of discussion, we co-create a classroom focus that students are happy to focus on.

## Teaching Students *How* to Drive the Work of Reading, Writing, and Thinking

Much of the driving course we design for our students is the curriculum we teach. Chapter 5 will talk more about how to turn a required curriculum into a small set of clear learning goals—each with learning progressions for students to travel. But our students need more from us than clear learning goals to really be able to drive on their own successfully. We need to teach them some basic strategies that they will use again and again to make learning truly theirs—strategies that underpin their reading work, their writing work, their conversation with each other, and even how they

decide for themselves what final grades they will select. Strategies that keep *us* out of their way while they do the most important work. They need to practice—again and again—how to make meaning on their own from complexity, thereby building skills they can use to make sense of their own life experiences beyond our classrooms and into the future.

A Three Step Meaning Making Process grounds the strategies presented in the next four chapters of this book [Figure 1.2]. From the start, this process hinges on what *students* are thinking. Because step one *always* starts with what students themselves are noticing, the end result of the process is meaning that students create on their own. It's learning that matters to them. Realizations that they drove themselves to. Understanding that they are proud of because *they* built it rather than simply parroting back what their teacher told them was important.

The most important outcome of anchoring our instruction in this Three Step Meaning Making Process is that it keeps us honest about keeping out of our students' way. It helps us ensure that we are not doing the most important thinking work for them. *Students* need to build their reading, writing, conversation, and self-reflection skills in our classroom so they can deploy those skills to navigate the very real complexity of their lives.

Step one in the meaning-making process is to ***start small***: what are some small details in the text that you are noticing? Or small things about your writing? Or small thoughts you're having that you could share with others? Or small moments along your learning journey that might help you to think about your growth? This is a safe, low-stakes place to start with anything complex—just pause to notice what you notice and capture what you think about it.

Step two is to begin to ***seek connections***: do you see any connections across the small details you've collected—about a text, about your own writing, about what you and your classmates have spoken of, about the notable moments in your learning journey? Or what if you tried sharing your thinking with others? Or sought a mentor text that connects somehow with what you've written and offers you some inspiration for making your writing stronger? What bigger ideas are forming based on any of these connections? Here is where students move from simply noticing what is in front of them to constructing meaning via the connections they can find.

Step three is where students ***take action*** they decide what they have learned and what they will do with it—something big or small, formal or

informal. Perhaps they'll use what they've figured out about a text as the foundation for a piece of writing. Perhaps they'll use what they've figured out about their own writing as a plan for revision. Perhaps they'll use what they've figured out from talking with each other to solve a shared problem or decide on a solution. Perhaps they'll use what they've figured out about their learning toward the goals they set for themselves to select the final grade that captures the true essence of their efforts. Whatever the case, that final piece in the process is something *students* own because *they* built it. The meaning they make is theirs, not their teacher's. As a result, the learning they've done lasts.

| **Steps in Meaning Making Process** | **Reading strategies to teach (Chapter 2)** | **Writing strategies to teach (Chapter 3)** | **Talk strategies to teach (Chapter 4)** | **Grading and assessment strategies to teach (Chapter 5)** | |
|---|---|---|---|---|---|
| | | | | **To set learning goals** | **To monitor progress** |
| **ONE:** | OTAs (original thought annotations) | Writer's memos | Conversation prep tasks | Self-evaluating on course learning progressions | Weekly reflection on student-selected learning goals |
| **TWO:** | Rambling thoughts<br><br>Concept mapping | Mentor text study<br><br>Reader feedback | Small group conversation | Examining assessment data to determine what to work on | Self-evaluating toward grade guidelines and choosing areas to improve in the time ahead |
| **THREE:** | Write? Speak? Present? Discuss? Make something? | Make a plan for revision and revise | Whole class conversation | Plans for learning and growth | Re-evaluating on course learning progressions to determine growth.<br><br>Grade letter/story to select a final grade |

Figure 1.2 Three Step Meaning Making Process
This chart shows the student-driven strategies that the following chapters will present, lined up with the Three Step Meaning Making Process.

## Cultivating Student Agency Above All Else

There's a story about me as a toddler that I don't remember but have heard many times. My family went to the mountains to stay in a cabin and do some fishing for a week or so. One morning, I took too long to answer my mom's question about what I wanted to wear, so she chose for me. And I flipped out. In true toddler fashion, I cried over and over and over that I wanted to wear my "engineers." I mean blue-and-white-striped OshKosh overalls—who wouldn't want to wear those? The story goes that my mom simply responded, "Well, Sarah, tomorrow when I ask you what you want to wear, tell me or I will have to choose for you."

This was my first lesson about agency.

My mom honored my agency—even as a toddler—by asking me what I wanted to wear. *And* she taught me how important it is to exercise my agency or someone else might step in there and make important decisions *for* me. I'm not sure if this interaction is the root or not of my career-long obsession to craft a classroom that orbits on student agency, but I've always sought agency in my own life and responded by pretty much shutting down when people take it from me.

Like when one of my high school English teachers told me that my interpretation of a section of *Gulliver's Travels* was flat-out wrong even though I could support it with evidence from the text. I'm sure my fuzzy teenage memory has forgotten the caring way my teacher actually responded, but it felt as if she were saying, "I don't care if you can support it with evidence from the text or not, Sarah. You're wrong." I certainly remember my frustration when it seemed my agency to pursue what *I* thought about a book was not the centerpiece of my experience as a student in her classroom. Though I used that experience to justify why I didn't read a single book that year, it's also my explanation for why, over the nearly three decades of my career, I've obsessed over how to centralize my students' agency to read and think and write.

But there needs to be a balance. Too much room to choose—especially in a classroom—can be paralyzing. Students need to build the skills to be able to learn from the journeys they might design for themselves, and they need support from us along the way to do this. The more I've focused on really, truly helping my students steer their own agency as learners, the more I've realized how carefully I must build a classroom experience for them—a driving course, if you will—where they can practice and exercise their agency. Which choices might they make themselves? When? Where? About what? In what context should those choices exist? What supports might I offer to bolster the success of those self-driven decisions? How narrow or wide should the range of choices be to inspire their highest success? How do I show them what the actual work looks like as they act on their own decisions about what to read, what to write, and what to think about it all? And how do I make sure that the work my students are doing in the learning environment I've built for them is actually moving them forward in the curriculum or standards I'm expected to teach?

As you know, it is complex, challenging design work. This book clarifies some of that work, offering simple tools to help you put your students out front, driving their reading, writing, and thinking work in a way that still gives you confidence they are truly growing.

CHAPTER 2

# INVITE STUDENTS TO DRIVE AS READERS

"What do you notice in this poem?"

I'm working with a class of sophomores, and we're looking at Jennifer Espinoza's poem "Things Haunt." The reading curricular goal we're addressing is about deriving bigger meaning from individual words and phrases in a literary text. It's our fifth day of class together in August, so I've only just met these students, and I don't know yet what kinds of readers they are.

But I know what kinds of readers I want them to become.

I want these students to build their reading confidence, to face a difficult text head-on, to know that they can derive meaning from complexity. More importantly, I want them to do this on their own, without a teacher explaining everything to them. Here at the start of the school year, I know I have to do *some* guiding. But I am also careful to open up spaces for my students to step in with their own ideas.

After I read the poem aloud, students take a few silent moments to zero in on specific words and phrases that seem important to them, writing on sticky notes to hold their thinking with two simple sentence starters: "I notice..." and "I think...." I've invited them into the first step of the Three Step Meaning Making Process. Notice how this starts in a simple, low-stakes place: what do you notice?

After five minutes or so, they share their notes with the other students sitting at their table. Tentative chatter fills the room. I'm anxious because poetry can be challenging, and they don't yet know each other well. Will they risk sharing their thoughts?

I secretly eavesdrop, and they *are* discussing their ideas about the poem. Confidence builds as they talk to each other, so it's time for some whole-class conversation.

"Is there a group that might tell us what you're talking about? What did you notice in the poem?"

"We noticed that the speaker seems to be struggling with identity."

"What words got you there?" I ask.

"Lines 6 and 7."

"Yeah," from another table. "Those lines made us wonder if the speaker was working against some expectations that society had that didn't quite fit."

"What else did you notice?" I ask, inviting space for more of their ideas to tumble into.

"What does it mean when a planet is in retrograde?"

I know from eavesdropping that one group had looked up this reference from the poem while they were talking. "It means that the movement of the planet makes it look like it's moving backward when it's actually moving forward," one student reads from his laptop screen.

"And some humans on Earth also think that we have a difficult time making sense of things when certain planets are in retrograde," I add, a tidbit I had discovered in my own quick internet search.

A few students chime in:

"So is the speaker having a hard time making sense of their identity?"

"Or are others having a hard time making sense of the speaker's identity?"

"Do others think the speaker is moving backward when they're actually moving forward?"

Rather than answering their questions, I listen and decide it might be the right moment to share what they don't yet know about the poet.

"According to the poet's bio, she's transgender." I want to keep the conversation focused on my students' growing ideas, so I'm careful to keep my thinking out of it. I continue, "We can't necessarily assume that the poet

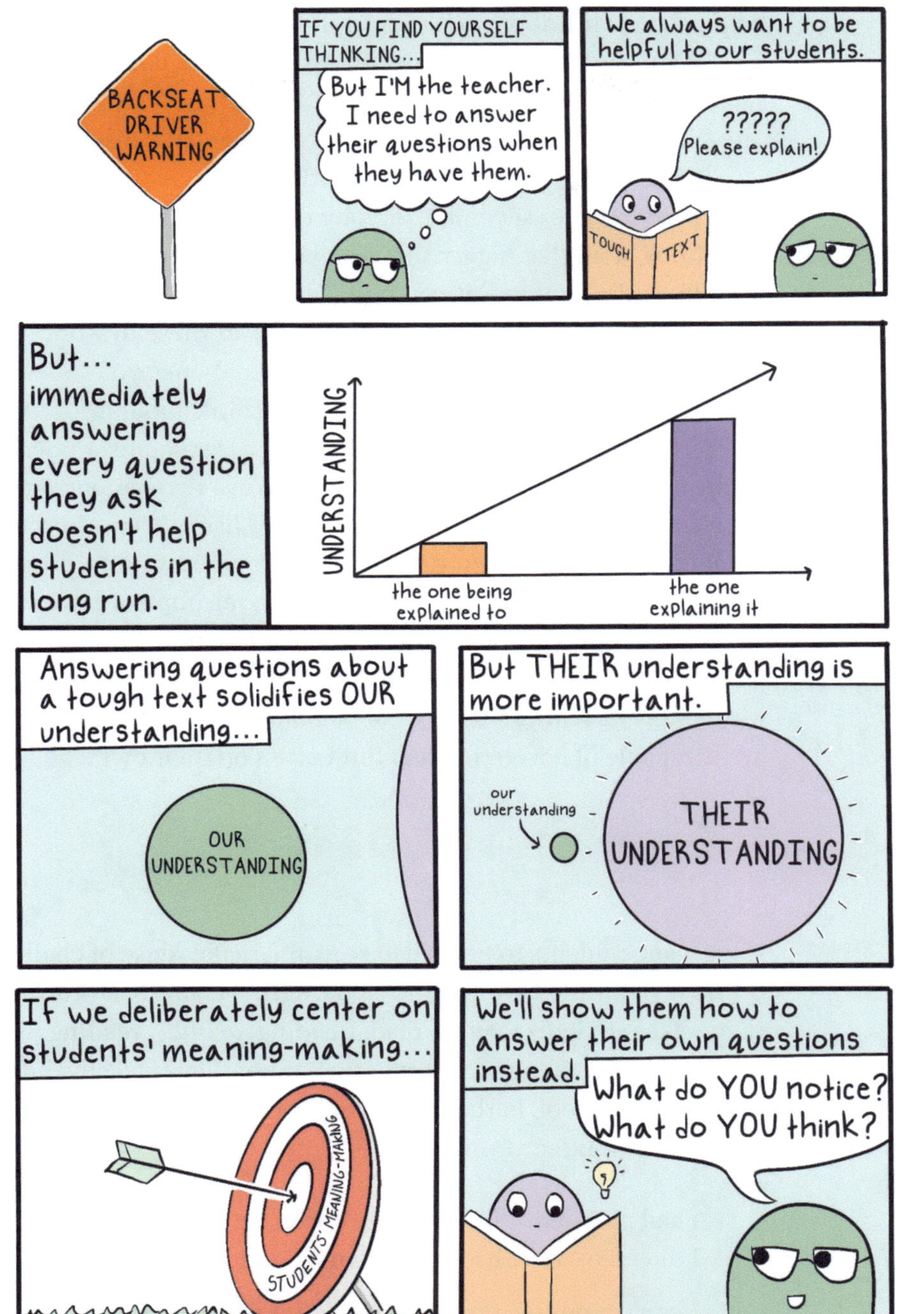


**Figure 2.1** Backseat Driver Warning

is the speaker in a poem, but how does knowing about the poet's identity help you to think about your questions about the poem?"

"We noticed with the repeated words in the last stanza, it seems the speaker wants people to listen."

"What do you think the speaker wants people to listen to?" I ask.

"What it feels like to live her identity?"

The room goes silent as everyone thinks for a few beats.

"Look at all that bigger thinking you built together by simply starting with the individual words you noticed and what you thought about them. Try again with another poem. Choose one of these to work on with your group, and share with us what you discovered once you've had some time to focus on what you notice and what you think about it."

To start this lesson, I simply handed my students a poem and a few sticky notes along with a brief invitation to use two sentence stems. I could have started with the poet's bio, or with a list of terms in the poem that students might not already know, or with a question to prompt them to look for words and phrases that repeat, for example. I have offered those types of supports in the past in the hope of helping my students approach a complex text with more confidence. But I've seen time and again that the kind of pre-teaching I used to do actually teaches our students that they are incapable of navigating text difficulties on their own.

## How Can We Invite Students to Drive as Readers?

If we want students to be able to read and make sense of challenging texts on their own, then we have to make sure we approach reading in a way that makes students *want* to read. Reading, *actually* reading, is hard work.

I can recall asking a class whether or not they typically did the reading assigned for school. Perhaps some of the comments from that conversation will sound familiar to you:

> I had no interest in any of the books we were assigned, and the books I did enjoy were brought down by mindless analysis.
>
> I can't pinpoint the time in my life where I stopped reading, probably around the time I started having to annotate. I felt as though I

> no longer could read for the sake of reading, instead I found myself skimming and scanning the pages to find seemingly "important" details that my teachers wanted to see for credit.
>
> I have felt like there was no hope for me to ever understand the words on the page.
>
> I wanted to go back to when I didn't have to have at least two annotations on each page to get full credit for my work. I wanted to find the meaning on my own.

These students had learned that their job was to listen for their teachers' meaning making and to return those ideas on exams and in essays. This job didn't require reading books.

What we really want for our students is for them to construct and revise meaning as they read. Sheridan Blau (2003) argues that reading is essentially rereading: "The reading of any difficult text will entail drafting and revision (largely in the reader's head) [...] Just as writing may be defined as rewriting, so is any reading worth doing essentially a process of rereading" (53).

And we want students to wonder, "Who am I? What might I become? What is this world in which I find myself? How might it be changed for the better?" (Edmundson, 2004, 5). We want them to read to make sense of their life experiences, to get to know themselves better, to imagine the experiences of others, and to imagine ways to make a better world (Greene, 1995; Rosenblatt, 1938/1995; Sumara, 2002; Witherall, 1991; Bruner, 2002; Nussbaum, 1995). We want them to be able to make meaning on their own.

Of course we want our students to learn what's important about the texts they read in our classes. But if we alone decide the topics to discuss with a particular text, we narrow the range of what's possible. I can recall the day a group of my students chose the lens of Biblical allusions when discussing Ralph Ellison's *Invisible Man*. It was not a lens I had already considered for the class's work with the book, but in the majority Christian community in which I was teaching, it was an area of expertise for the students. They tapped into their knowledge and out flowed interpretations and insights that I did not expect. If we make decisions for students about what is important in a text, they never have the opportunity to show us what they can do.

Yet, we ourselves often impede this kind of reading. We get in the way when we make reading about right answers on quizzes rather than exploring ideas. When we decide what to discuss with each text rather than seeing what our students are interested in talking about. When we attach points or grades to the work students do with the reading. When we fill up class time with teacher-directed tasks and leave no space for students. I have done all these things myself toward the goal of simplifying complex work in my classroom. I've done all of these things because it seemed like that was what I was supposed to do—it's what *my* teachers did, and many of these practices are still common today.

But we've all seen (or perhaps experienced ourselves as students) what happens to readers when we control their meaning-making process. Many give up on reading. I remember experiences in high school of either not reading or—if I did keep up with the assigned reading—doing so without joy or wonder or curiosity or a purpose that mattered to me. Still, despite experiences like this as a student myself in classrooms where my teachers didn't let me drive my own reading, I have asked my students to read with a single-minded focus toward what *I* deemed important about the texts I assigned.

Instead of designing elaborate systems to *check up* on readers, we can consider what we can do to *support* their reading. We can use the Three Step Meaning Making Process [see Figure 2.2] to invite students to make choices that enable them to grow their ownership over the ideas that they are constructing as they read. Every choice we offer students is an invitation for them to develop more ownership over their work.

Using the Three Step Meaning Making Process to guide our reading instruction may not always look fancy, and it may not consistently give you and me a platform to share our own insight about a text, but it *does* teach kids how to read any kind of text deeply, critically, and with engagement.

The opening story in this chapter shows the first step of this process using a short poem, but the process works equally well with longer texts and texts we often consider "difficult." Recently, as a class was completing work with Faulkner's *As I Lay Dying* while using these strategies, a student told me that she literally dropped the book in frustration when she read the final sentence. She had traced what she noticed about the characters' journeys, desires, and conflicts on original thought annotations (OTAs).

| Meaning-making process step | | Reading strategies to teach | Choice points we can offer students |
|---|---|---|---|
| ONE: | • What are your initial ideas? | Original Thought Annotations (OTAs) | → when to pause and write an OTA<br>→ what to focus on with each OTA |
| TWO: | • Grow your thinking across your ideas. | Rambling thoughts<br>Concept mapping<br>Two-page spreads<br>Small group shared work | → which OTAs to use for rambling thoughts<br>→ what ideas to explore in rambling thoughts<br>→ how to structure a concept map<br>→ what to focus on in a two-page spread<br>→ what to focus on with a small group |
| THREE: | • Decide what you've figured out about the text and do something with it. | Write? Speak? Present? Discuss? Make something? | → how to communicate ideas built about the text |

Figure 2.2 Three Step Meaning Making Process for Reading Strategies

She had used rambling thoughts and concept mapping to form bigger ideas about her hope for the characters along the way. But the ending betrayed all of that for her.

Unless you've been fully immersed in a text, you can't drop it in disgust or throw it across the room or burst out in tears of joy or laugh uncontrollably (or have to drop your oatmeal spoon so you could cry a little, as was the case for me when I finally read Hinton's *The Outsiders* a few years ago). There are many voices in the world today that try to tell us that this intensity, this ability to fully respond to the text, isn't necessary—or even isn't possible—in school. That our aim in school is academic strength. But we know that the opposite is true: engagement with the text sparks and sustains the kind of analysis and insights that we often label as academic strengths. We can teach in a way that nourishes both engagement and analysis.

## *Start Small*: Teach Students to Use Original Thought Annotations to Capture Their Initial Ideas Based on the Small Things They Notice

I often remind my students that "If anything is odd, inappropriate, confusing, or boring, it's probably important" (Rex & McEachen, 1999). We can teach students that when they come up against an unknown or a surprise or just something that makes them scratch their head, they can use a sticky note to record the page number, the thing they noticed in the text, and the thought they had about it. Start with modeling. Read a text together and point out one thing *you* noticed and wondered about. Show them what you would write on a sticky note. Make sure it's a simple, small thing, so students know it's okay to start with something small. Then invite them to point out the small things *they've* noticed and wondered about. Once they've captured this thinking on the sticky note, they can put it on the

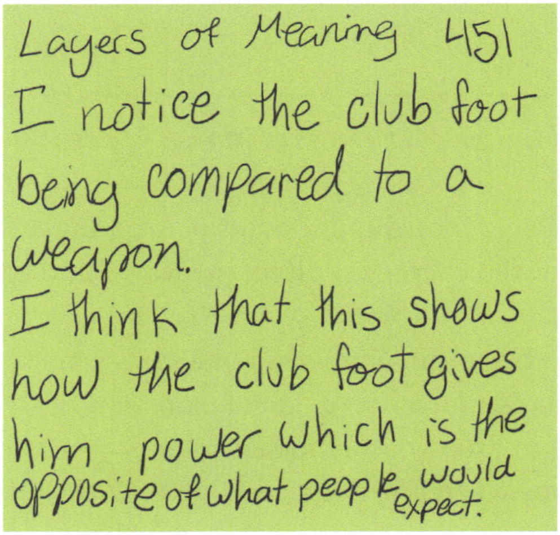

Layers of Meaning 451
I notice the club foot being compared to a weapon.
I think that this shows how the club foot gives him power which is the opposite of what people would expect.

**Figure 2.3** Lucia's OTA Eleventh grader, Lucia, stopped to make a note about a character's club foot in Flannery O'Connor's short story, "The Lame Shall Enter First." "451" is the page number where Lucia had the thought. "Layers of Meaning" refers to one of the categories for OTAs I offer my International Baccalaureate Literature classes. It's a broad category that encompasses symbolism and figurative language. I offer a list of categories for students' OTAs to focus their eyes a bit on noticings that will help them with the literary analytic task of the class. With this single OTA, Lucia is beginning to develop her ideas about O'Connor's methods of characterization.

page that inspired the thought or add it to a collection of OTAs on a page in their notebook. Figures 2.3 and 2.4 show OTAs from my students, Lucia and Jake.

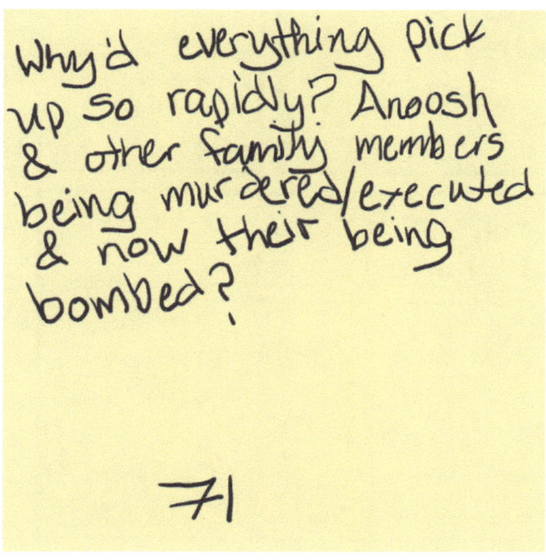


**Figure 2.4** Jake's OTA Tenth grader, Jake, stopped to wonder about the pace of the plot in Marjane Satrapi's memoir, *Persepolis*. Though he first wrote what he was thinking with his question about why things had picked up so rapidly, he followed that with what he noticed—the plot events that had happened in quick succession. "71" is the page number where Jake had the thought. The categories I gave Jake's class came from the list in Figure 2.6.

The humble sticky note is a small container, just enough room for one noticing and a few thoughts about it. This routine shows our students there is a safe place to start whenever they run across something unknown, unexpected, or confusing when reading—ask yourself: *What do you notice?* and *What do you think about it?*

Once students have had opportunities to simply notice what they notice, we can sharpen their noticing with options that focus their eyes a bit more. We might identify the skills our students still need to develop and then connect what they notice to those skills (Roberts, 2018). Or we can look for skills and strategies that will enrich our students as readers, like Beers and Probst provide in their *Notice and Note* books (2012, 2016) or like Marilyn Pryle's (2018) reading response categories in *Reading with Presence*. My go-to list [Figure 2.6] is something my colleagues and I have

BACKSEAT
DRIVER
WARNING

IF YOU FIND YOURSELF THINKING...
I don't think my students will know what to focus on in a book if I don't give them a list of questions ahead of time.

CONSIDER...
We might want to help focus student's thinking as they approach a tough text...

...to make it simpler and easier for them to identify what's most important.
IMPORTANT ELEMENTS
of our TOUGH
TEXT

But when we do that ahead of time as we plan our teaching, we do the most important thinking for our students...

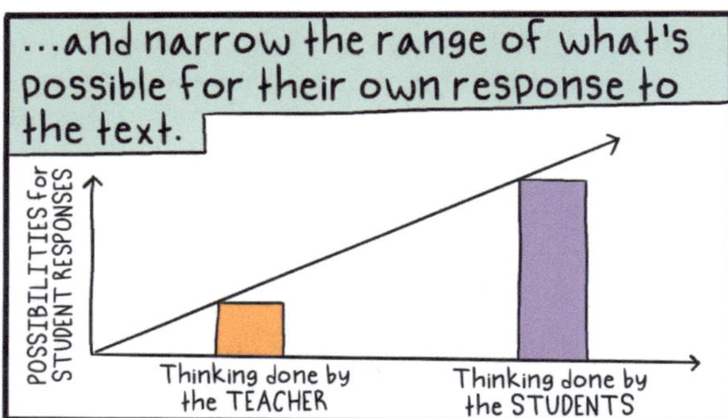
...and narrow the range of what's possible for their own response to the text.
POSSIBILITIES for STUDENT RESPONSES
Thinking done by the TEACHER
Thinking done by the STUDENTS

We can work together with our students to determine what about any text we spend class time on...

what do YOU think is important for us to talk about?

...which goes a long way toward showing them their
IDEAS MATTER!
I think...

**Figure 2.5** Backseat Driver Warning

worked on and added to over the years. It started with a list of topics for "minute papers" from Linda Nilson's *Creating Self-Regulated Learners* (2013, 28). I turn to it when I am looking for a lens that will help students to consider a text in a new light or to deepen their thinking.

1. An idea or moment you think is **important**.
2. Something **useful or valuable** that you learned.
3. Something **surprising** - an idea, event, statistic, or thing a person does or says.
4. Anything you notice that **occurs more than once**.
5. Any **emotional reactions** you're having as you read.
6. Something that seems to have **deeper meaning**: a symbol, metaphor, allusion...
7. Things that are **confusing**.
8. Anything that **helps or hinders your understanding**.
9. Ideas or actions you want to **make use of in your life**.
10. Material that lines up with or challenges **what you already know**.
11. Material that relates to **what you're studying in other classes**.
12. A **question** you have or something that **answers** a question you have.
13. Anything the text makes you **wonder** about.
14. **Something you can explain** because you now understand it well.
15. **Conflicts, contrasts, or contradictions** - in ideas, in the actions/words of people...
16. Any **predictions** you have about what might happen later in the text.
17. A sentence or paragraph that **wows you** because of how it's written.
18. A **new word** that you think is interesting.
19. How the text helps you to think about **what you could write about**.
20. **Free choice** - anything that jumps out at you for whatever reason.

**Figure 2.6** Invitations for Students' OTAs

The list works for novels or memoirs or poetry, film or nonfiction, books or newspaper articles, even a social media post or a meme. You can give students the whole list or just a few items, depending on the text, the curriculum, and their needs as readers. If we provide a list of specific things we've already noticed in the text ourselves, we end up doing the thinking for our students. We want to build students' capacities to be independent, to do the thinking work on their own. So a generic list of what they *could* notice is powerful because students choose what about the text to pay attention to themselves. Such a list can focus them before they read or can act as a filter to identify what they're thinking after they've read. Either way, this keeps the work centered on students' meaning making. Rather than the comprehension questions I used in the past to guide students' reading—or the reading quizzes I used to hold them accountable for doing the reading to begin with—this strategy offers lenses or ideas that students can learn to use with *any* text to help them uncover what *they* notice and what they think about it.

## *Seek Connections*: Teach Students to Connect Their Ideas to Grow Their Thinking

Once students collect several ideas about the text by focusing on what they notice and what they think about it, give them space to pull their ideas together into something more.

Say I've been reading Jesmyn Ward's *Salvage the Bones*, and I've noticed several times that the narrator, Esch, describes all of the mothers in her life: Mama (dead for about eight years now), China (her brother's dog who has recently birthed puppies), Medea (from the Jason and Medea myth), and Hurricane Katrina (Mother Nature). I might grab the sticky notes where I recorded those noticings and write to make connections across them, exploring what Esch's descriptions of these mothers suggest about what she thinks about her own impending motherhood.

I'll bet you've been through a similar process where you've thought a lot about a text you want to understand better. However, our students may never have had the luxury of time and space in school to think about their reading in this way, or perhaps they haven't been taught to value and build these connections. We can do that now.

### *Rambling Thoughts*

One strategy to teach students to seek connections to grow their thinking is to invite some rambling writing. This is an opportunity for them to develop their thinking about the patterns they've noticed and the connections they've made in their reading. It's a chance to just get the ideas out of their heads and follow them wherever the words take them, where it's safe to take risks, to be tentative, to be uncertain about their thinking.

Begin by asking students to move a handful of their sticky note noticings onto a left-side page in their writer's notebook—very much like Kate Roberts's (2018) approach of "long writing" about a text to pull together ideas based on a selection of annotations (113–18). Then, have them use the opposite page to ramble about the connections that exist between the noticings they've chosen. By "ramble," I explain to students that I mean they should write to follow their ideas without worrying about spelling or punctuation or sentence structure. This might feel very different to our students from other writing they have previously done in school, so it can be helpful to explain that rambling writing helps us to figure out what we're thinking. Show them an example from a past student, or do some rambling writing in front of them on the big screen in the room, thinking aloud as you write.

- What is this about?
- What happens next?
- What does it look like, feel like, smell like?
- How can I restate that?
- What's my reaction to that?
- What example or experience can I call up to illustrate that?
- What parts of my prior reading can I bring to bear on that?
- What comparison can I make that makes that clearer?
- Why does that matter?
- What do I mean by that?
- Who else would agree with that? Disagree?
- How can I qualify that statement? What are the exceptions?
- How does that fit into larger debates or controversies? (Newkirk, 2017, pp. 143-4)

**Figure 2.7** Questions to Ask to Push Your Thinking as You Ramble

I model by first writing the topic I'll be rambling about at the top of the blank right page. Then, I work to make sense of what I've noticed, thinking aloud as I write. I show how I keep writing until I've either filled the page or run out of time. Students see that my thinking may be rough, and my writing may be messy. I include evidence once or twice as I write, and I suggest to students that they do the same when they write. I also share a helpful list of prompts from Tom Newkirk that, while not written for text analysis, have proven helpful for me and for my students in this work [Figure 2.7]. It's worth giving each student a copy of this list to tape it into their notebooks—it's that good.

After the demo, it's the students' turn. Put about ten minutes (or less) on the timer for their first go at rambling writing, but plan to work up over time to rambling for twenty to thirty minutes or more.

Students can ramble their way into bigger ideas about the reading that they might not have discovered otherwise. It can help them discover their *own* superpowers as readers and thinkers. And if the risks rambling writers take while pushing their thinking deeper *don't* end up getting them anywhere interesting, no worries. It's just rambling.

Consider Suriya's rambling about Chapter 6 of *The Great Gatsby* [Figure 2.8], which she and her book club chose to read together. (Note—Suriya completed this rambling electronically rather than in her notebook. I didn't ask students to keep paper notebooks during online/hybrid school of the 2020–1 school year.)

> Its literally hilarious how in love nick is with gatsby, like he spent 5 out of 10 pages in this chapter describing him romantically and sentimentally, and he has some resentment towards Daisy for being the object of that affection
>
> Also its interesting how its considered totally normal for tom to have "a girl in New York" but when he finds out that she knows someone that he doesnt, he gets upset and thinks hes giving her too much freedom like what kind of bullshit
>
> Also west egg is super personified in this chapter through both nick and daisy's eyes. Its sort of a bubble of upper class white people who are very.. fluffy? Idk the word im looking for here OH its frivolous they dont care about real issues and concern themselves with rumors about gatsby and dinners and stuff like that
>
> Hmmm what else i started reading ch 7 and the way the characters react to the heat is really something else and gatsby going into this weird, depressive? state bc of daisy
>
> Also his obsession with recreating the past perfectly is super unhealthy lmao
>
> Im curious about daisys reaction to the party bc apparently she didnt enjoy any of it except when she was with gatsby so is it the frivolity? The drunkenness? I thought she liked gatsbys lifestyle but OHHH thats why he changed it so suddenly in the next chapter bc she didnt like his lifestyle so he changed it to something he thought shed like better and nick realizes this which is why he doesnt like it and thats manifested in his dislike of the butler who was "rude" to him its like a symbol of how he feels about gatsby changing himself for daisy bc hes in love with the gatsby he met not the gatsby that daisys in love with
>
> Also gatsbys 'old sport' thing might have some hidden meaning idk, from what i remember he only calls nick old sport which is like 👀 yknow
>
> Why did tom go with the polo/ athlete thing at first? Did he like it or was he just tired of saying it was wrong? Cos then he goes back into 'oblivion' or whatever
>
> Also its so funny how gatsby and daisy keep asking nick to be there while they make googly eyes at each other poor nick is just like :))))) it really is that meme
>
> Dkjgshkjlgshkdj ok thats all i got i guess but i wanna say im really rooting for nick and gatsby to end up together i dont think its gonna happen but im sure theres a fanfic about it somewhere

**Figure 2.8** Suriya's Rambling About Chapter 6 of *The Great Gatsby*

This is rambling writing. Suriya told me later that she typed this with her thumbs on a Google Doc on her phone. So it's messy, yes. But engaged and insightful. Of course we want our students' writing to be mechanically sound so they are able to clearly communicate their ideas. But rambling writing is for the writer, not for an audience. If we focused only on the errors in this insightful piece of writing, we would miss that Suriya is rambling her way to a unique and well-supported interpretation of *Gatsby*.

Rambling invites students to write to figure out what they are thinking, to discover rather than to communicate. To write for themselves. Free of pressure to write "correctly," writing can become liberating space to explore ideas—brilliant ideas that might not surface otherwise.

Get students used to trying on ideas by giving them lots of opportunities to ramble in writing—at least once a week or once every other week. You can use a bit of rambling as a warm-up for whole-class discussion or as a precursor for small group conversation. Asking group members to read their ramblings to the group and consider common threads with others' ideas can launch strong discussions.

### Concept Mapping

Another powerful strategy that teaches students how to seek connections to grow their thinking is concept mapping (adapted from Nilson, 2013). Students (individually or in groups) start by making a list of concepts from the texts that they find important—for example, they may include characters, moments, conflicts, symbols, topics, rhetorical strategies, examples, or claims. Then, students select what they each think is the central or overriding concept on the list. This becomes the focal point of the student's concept map, and it's often different for each student. They create a map to explore this central concept, drawing ideas from their own reading, from their OTAs, from their rambling writing, and from class discussions, arranging those ideas on the page to show how they connect. They make notations all over the map to indicate how the different concepts connect and relate. Students must choose for themselves which ideas to include. It's laser-focused on students' own meaning making. And their resulting maps can show (both them and us!) their strengths as thinkers.

Some students can make successful concept maps just with a set of instructions to follow. Others will need to watch you make one as you think aloud about what you're doing while others may just need examples to examine. But don't belabor the instructions. Students will understand concept mapping better once they've tried making one.

Let's take a look at two student examples, both about Jordan Peele's film, *Get Out*. Isabel [Figure 2.9] has used color to show that "control" is the dominant concept she's seeing in the film, with "hypnotism," "helplessness," "relationships," and "race" nested beneath and the remaining concepts as additional layers. What remains unresolved for her shows up in the list of questions. Isabel used this map to connect her individual noticings collected on OTAs as we watched the film in class. It seems she has a theory emerging—that Jordan Peele's horror-film take on race in America is ultimately about control. This is something she can explore more in conversations with her classmates and eventually in some sort of writing or presentation to solidify what she has figured out about the text.

Alex's map [Figure 2.10] shows how the same reading process—starting small with OTAs, then seeking connections across those ideas with a strategy like concept mapping—leads students to their own unique outcomes. Where Isabel focused on control as the driving factor in the film, Alex read *Get Out* as a direct treatise on race in America. Alex's concept map shows an evolving conversation that the film inspired in his thinking. He points out critical moments from the film, poses questions, and answers them.

Isabel's and Alex's maps reflect two different theories about the same text, but they both show thoughtful reading and genuine meaning making, work that each student did on their own, without me getting in the way or preventing them from developing their own ideas by preemptively sharing mine.

## *Other Step Two Strategies*

Rambling thoughts and concept mapping are only two possible strategies to teach students. There are certainly other ways students can learn to build their thinking by seeking connections across what they've noticed as they've read. Any task that invites students to look across individual OTAs from step one and start forging connections between them to grow thinking will work.

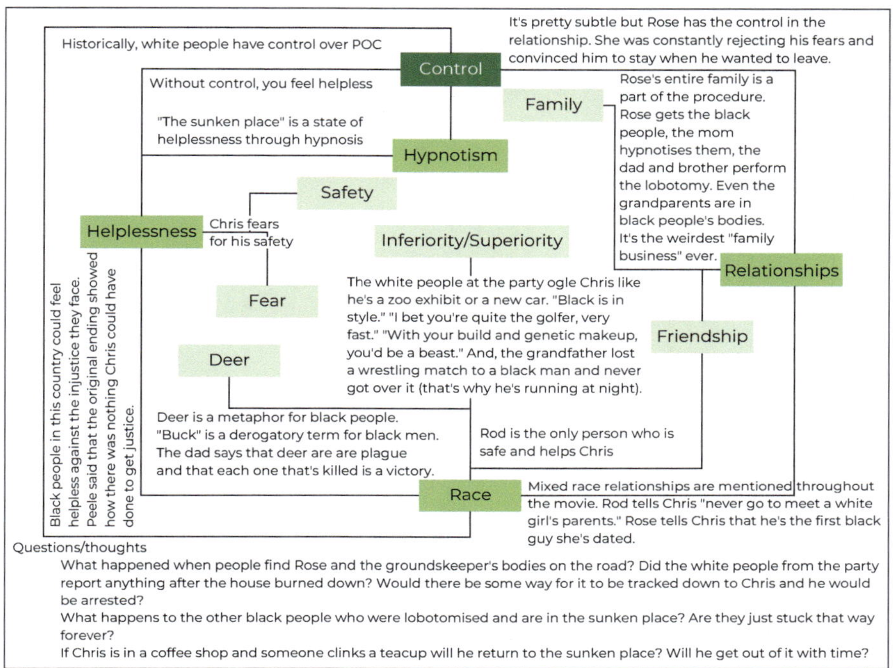

Historically, white people have control over POC
Control
It's pretty subtle but Rose has the control in the relationship. She was constantly rejecting his fears and convinced him to stay when he wanted to leave.
Without control, you feel helpless
Family
Rose's entire family is a part of the procedure. Rose gets the black people, the mom hypnotises them, the dad and brother perform the lobotomy. Even the grandparents are in black people's bodies. It's the weirdest "family business" ever.
"The sunken place" is a state of helplessness through hypnosis
Hypnotism
Safety
Helplessness
Chris fears for his safety
Inferiority/Superiority
Relationships
Black people in this country could feel helpless against the injustice they face. Peele said that the original ending showed how there was nothing Chris could have done to get justice.
Fear
The white people at the party ogle Chris like he's a zoo exhibit or a new car. "Black is in style." "I bet you're quite the golfer, very fast." "With your build and genetic makeup, you'd be a beast." And, the grandfather lost a wrestling match to a black man and never got over it (that's why he's running at night).
Friendship
Deer
Deer is a metaphor for black people. "Buck" is a derogatory term for black men. The dad says that deer are are plague and that each one that's killed is a victory.
Rod is the only person who is safe and helps Chris
Race
Mixed race relationships are mentioned throughout the movie. Rod tells Chris "never go to meet a white girl's parents." Rose tells Chris that he's the first black guy she's dated.
Questions/thoughts
What happened when people find Rose and the groundskeeper's bodies on the road? Did the white people from the party report anything after the house burned down? Would there be some way for it to be tracked down to Chris and he would be arrested?
What happens to the other black people who were lobotomised and are in the sunken place? Are they just stuck that way forever?
If Chris is in a coffee shop and someone clinks a teacup will he return to the sunken place? Will he get out of it with time?

**Figure 2.9** Isabel's Concept Map on *Get Out*

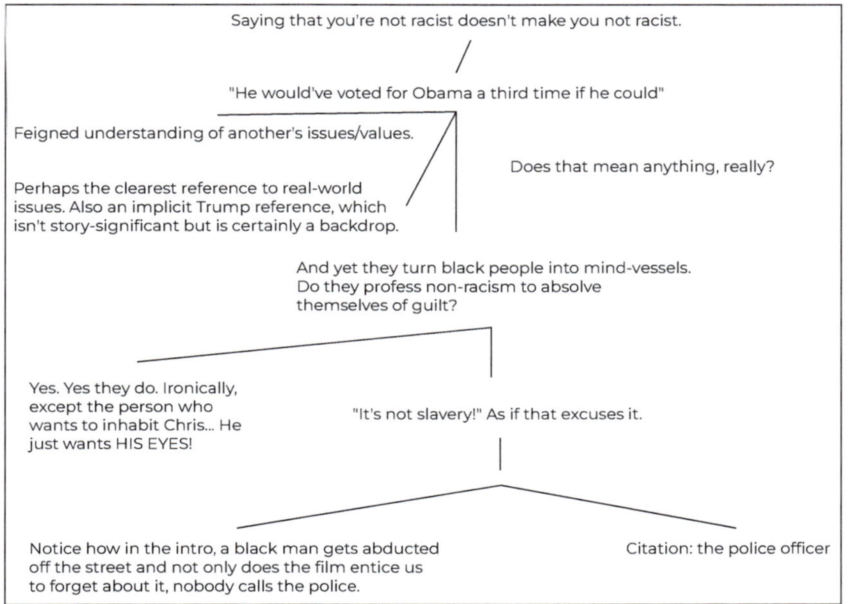

Saying that you're not racist doesn't make you not racist.
"He would've voted for Obama a third time if he could"
Feigned understanding of another's issues/values.
Does that mean anything, really?
Perhaps the clearest reference to real-world issues. Also an implicit Trump reference, which isn't story-significant but is certainly a backdrop.
And yet they turn black people into mind-vessels. Do they profess non-racism to absolve themselves of guilt?
Yes. Yes they do. Ironically, except the person who wants to inhabit Chris... He just wants HIS EYES!
"It's not slavery!" As if that excuses it.
Notice how in the intro, a black man gets abducted off the street and not only does the film entice us to forget about it, nobody calls the police.
Citation: the police officer

**Figure 2.10** Alex's Concept Map on *Get Out*

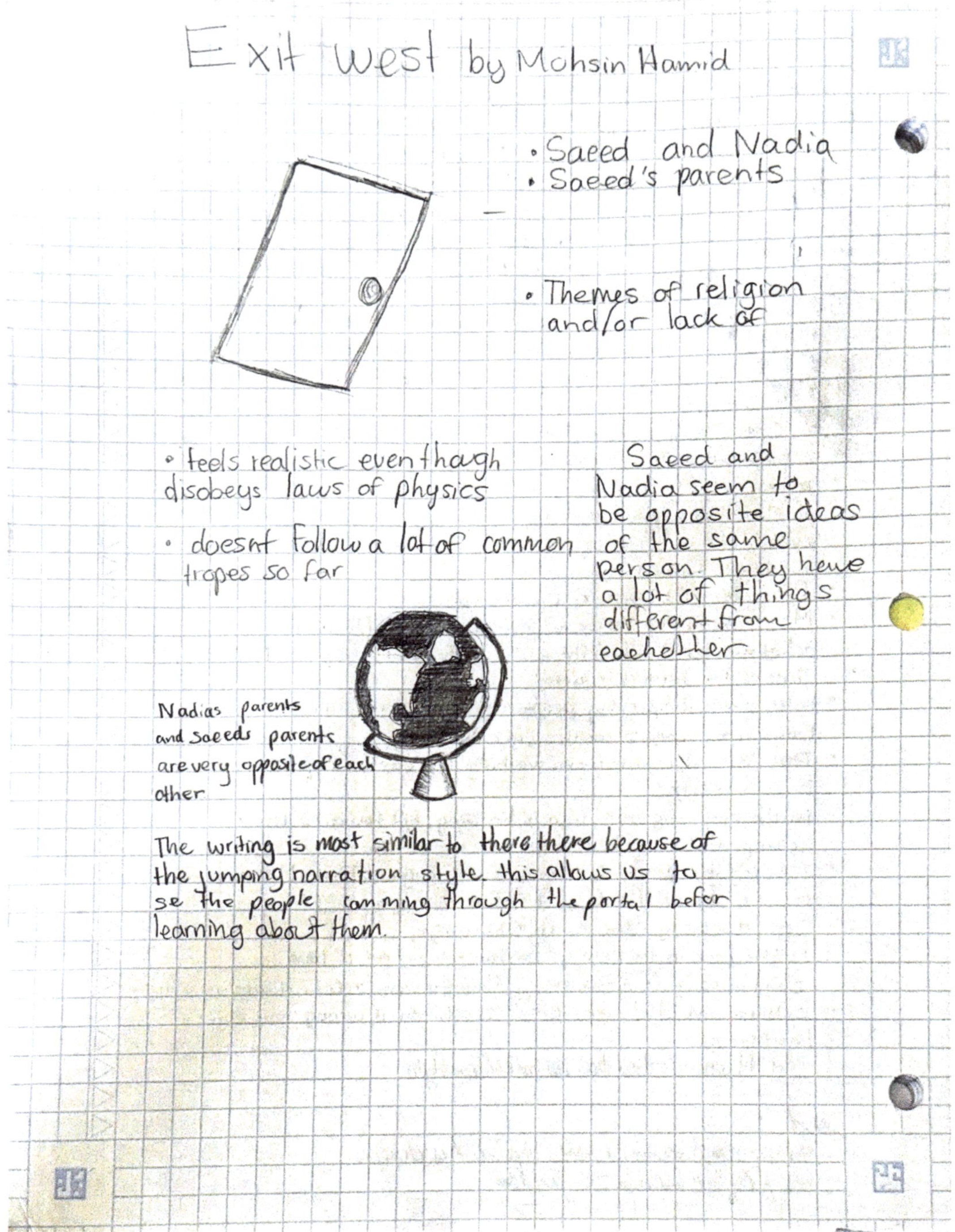

Exit West by Mohsin Hamid
• Saeed and Nadia
• Saeed's parents
• Themes of religion and/or lack of
• feels realistic even though disobeys laws of physics
• doesn't follow a lot of common tropes so far
Saeed and Nadia seem to be opposite ideas of the same person. They have a lot of things different from eachother
Nadias parents and saeeds parents are very opposite of each other
The writing is most similar to there there because of the jumping narration style. this allows us to se the people comming through the portal befor learning about them.


**Figure 2.11a** Oscar's Two-Page Spread (in process) on Mohsin Hamid's *Exit West*

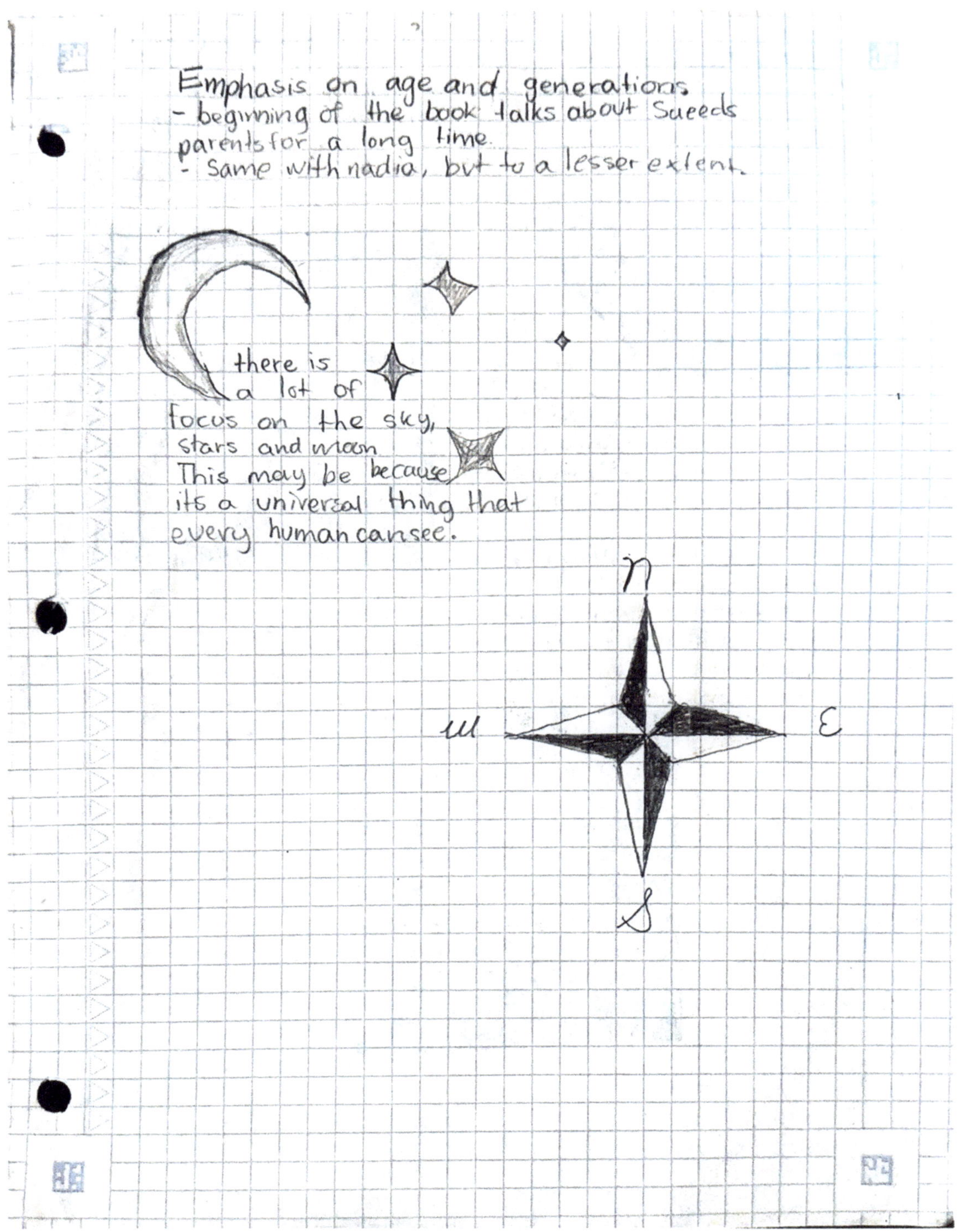
Emphasis on age and generations
- beginning of the book talks about Saeeds parents for a long time.
- Same with nadia, but to a lesser extent.
there is a lot of focus on the sky, stars and moon
This may be because its a universal thing that every human can see.
n
W
E
S

Figure 2.11b

### Two-Page Spreads

The *New York Times* offers resources on what they call "one-pagers" (Schulten, 2023). There are also ideas for using two-page spreads with book clubs in *4 Essential Studies* (Kittle & Gallagher, 2021). The idea is for students to use a template or a blank page to collect quotations, images, and thoughts from and about a particular text. I recently used two-page spreads as an invitation for my eleventh graders to pull together their thinking about their independent reading books. Figures 2.11 and 2.12 are two examples.

### Small-Group Shared Work

Students can work together with classmates to connect their ideas on shared documents. I set up a template slide deck for tenth-grade book groups, which they then used as they wished to collect their shared thinking as they read and discussed the book. Here are two slides in process from a group reading Petrus's *The Stars and the Blackness Between Them* [Figure 2.13]. You can see they are starting to collect the big topics their book was asking them to think about and the questions they had as they read. Other slides they worked on included a collection of important moments, a concept map, and a slide for them to think through their ideas about the overall theme of the text.

### Conversation

Conversation can be incredibly helpful for students as they work to grow their thinking across the small things they've noticed in a text. Ongoing, informal small-group conversation can be useful, for example: "Turn to a neighbor and share one OTA with each other. Talk to discover any connections in your thinking." More formal whole-class conversation can also be a fruitful place for students to grow thinking. (See Chapter 4 for some specific strategies.) Finally, do not underestimate the power of conversation with *you* to grow students' thinking. With intentional prompts in reading conferences, you can help students to build their ideas, for example: "Can you find two OTAs you've written that might be connected somehow? Explain the connection to me."

## *Take Action*: Tasks for Step Three in the Meaning Making Process

OTAs, rambling thoughts, and concept maps are not summative assessment tasks. They are rough thinking in development. They are stair steps from the tentative ideas that form in students' initial noticings and exploratory writing to the more confident stances students might take next as they move into step three of the meaning-making process. Here, invite students to take action—decide what they've figured out and do something with it. The possibilities are many: a piece of writing, a presentation, an artistic response, a formal class conversation... The step one and two tasks this chapter explores are tools to help students figure out what *they* know about a complex text, which makes for excellent preparation for a subsequent summative assessment you may invite in step three. I've used OTAs and concept maps effectively before timed essays about books in Advanced Placement Literature, for example, or as an entrance ticket into a seminar conversation that serves as a summative task (seminars do make great step two tasks, too—it's all about how you're inviting your students to *use* the work to further their thinking). My colleagues have started using concept maps for students to make sense of an entire semester's worth of thinking, reading, writing, and discussion in preparation to write to select their grade for the semester. Students could take a few different sets of rambling thoughts and mine them for a possible thesis for a longer paper or for the focus of a presentation.

Think about major tasks you already use in your classroom. How might you use OTAs and rambling thoughts and/or concept maps to invite students to drive toward those major tasks, making those same tasks true representations of the thinking and ideas your students can build on their own?

## A Quick Word About (Not) Grading and Assessment

As with anything students create, it's tempting to use a rubric to grade a concept map or some rambling writing or a collection of OTAs. I caution you not to. Even a "finished" concept map might need revision as a student's

Independent
reading book
from the rampant sexism and pretending and trauma of this world
Surfacing
water as birth and rebirth
emerging from society that calls Joe's attempted rape okay
repeated dives as healing attempt
lake diving when looking for rock paintings = rebirth from false memories
blurred vision of aborted fetus
"I couldn't accept it, that mutilation, ruin I'd made, I needed a different version" (143)
do we need to forgive to emerge like return to Joe
restorative justice of guilt of abortion
male power to persuade to get abortion → do men deserve say?
physical journey to childhood home
Characters
narrator
artist - animalistic
cares about nature -
nameless - reflective - hates US -
doesn't trust love - divorcée -
false memories - lacks emotion -
emotional journey towards Joe -
coping with pain of past
anna
married to David -
victimized by him -
must wear makeup which serves to
hide pain & cheating - can't fathom
siding against David - weaponizes
sex - lacks awareness - talkative -
copes through pretending
Joe
rejected by narrator -
initially content -
genuine love of narrator -
vet of Vietnam war - very quiet
david
film "random samples":
routinely assaults
anna - openly a cheater -
very controlling -
self-obsessed
cruel -
flirtation
with anna is performative -
hypocritically likes baseball
but "hates American"
sexist pig


Figure 2.12a Zachariah's Two-Page Spread on Margaret Atwood's *Surfacing*

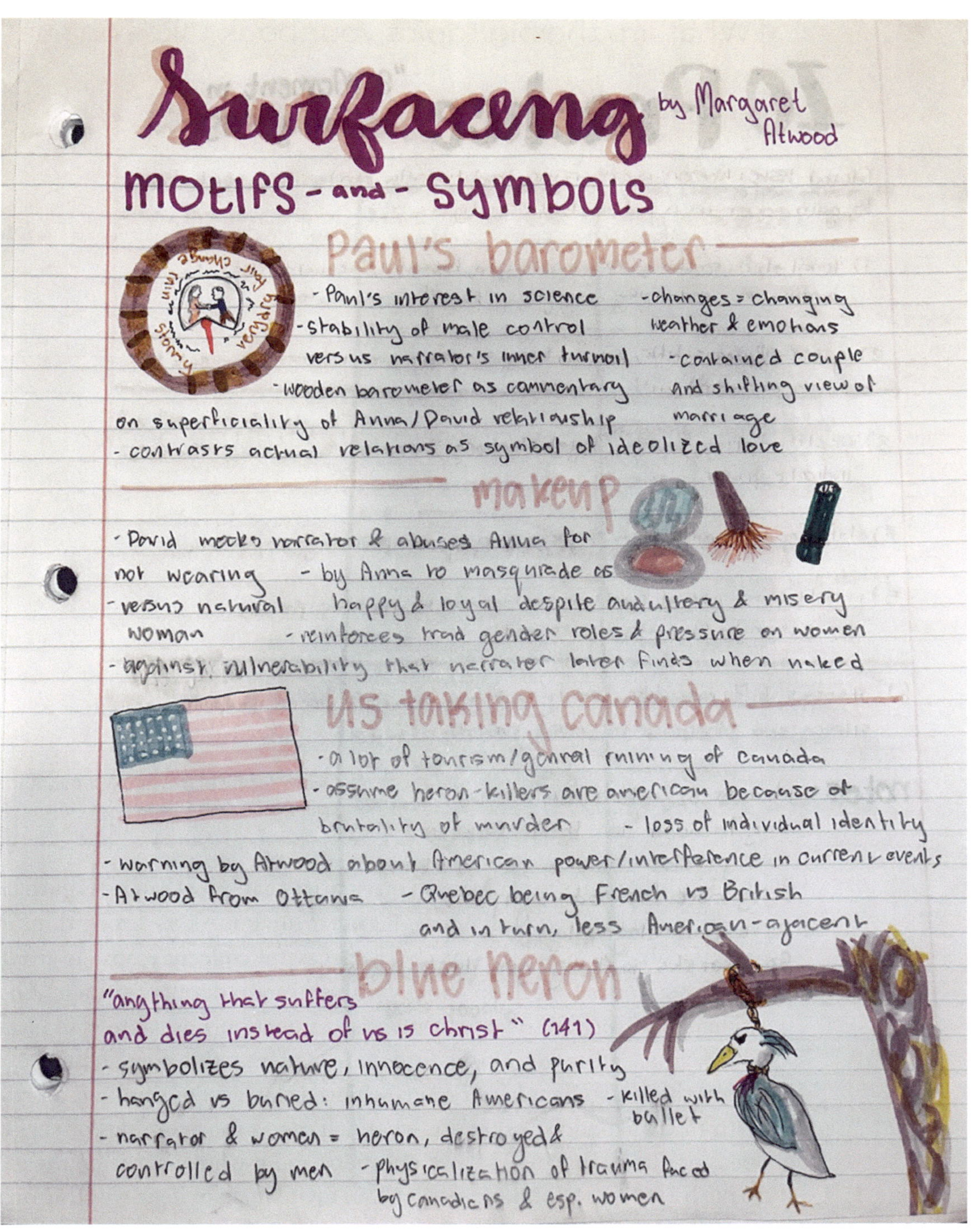
Surfacing by Margaret Atwood
motifs - and - symbols
Paul's barometer
- Paul's interest in science
- stability of male control versus narrator's inner turmoil
- wooden barometer as commentary on superficiality of Anna/David relationship
- contrasts actual relations as symbol of ideolized love
- changes = changing weather & emotions
- contained couple and shifting view of marriage
makeup
- David mocks narrator & abuses Anna for not wearing
- versus natural woman
- against vulnerability that narrator later finds when naked
- by Anna to masquerade as happy & loyal despite adultery & misery
- reinforces trad gender roles & pressure on women
us taking canada
- a lot of tourism/genral ruining of canada
- assume heron-killers are american because of brutality of murder
- loss of individual identity
- warning by Atwood about American power/interference in current events
- Atwood from Ottawa
- Quebec being French vs British and in turn, less American-ajacent
blue heron
"anything that suffers and dies instead of us is christ" (141)
- symbolizes nature, innocence, and purity
- hanged vs buried: inhumane Americans
- killed with ballet
- narrator & women = heron, destroyed & controlled by men
- physicalization of trauma faced by canadians & esp. women
Figure 2.12b

What are the big topics your book takes on?

1. Gender roles
2. Lost love
3. Rebirth
4. Coming of age
5. Family
6. Diverse queer representation
7. Astrology - There's a page of a star sign season everytime the season changes in the book
8. Facing reality
9. Religion
10. Cancer
11. Sickness
12. Peace

What are your questions about the book?
(and what ideas do you have in response to those questions as you keep reading?)

Does Aufa get justice?
Is Mabel going to get better?
Will Audre's mom ever make up with Audre?

**Figure 2.13** Shared Slides a Book Group Used to Record Their Thinking About Petrus's *The Stars and the Blackness Between Them*

thinking continues to evolve. You may notice that Isabel's map [Figure 2.9] is a bit more detailed than Alex's [Figure 2.10], but Alex's strong thinking is impossible to miss. They are both successful concept maps, as are the uber messy ones I see in notebooks with eraser marks all over them. Look at them only for your own formative assessment purposes—to plan future instruction and to get a peek into your students' thinking about a text. If you think a student hasn't quite achieved the level of thinking possible with their map, don't point out what you see as shortcomings or suggest ideas or directions. Instead, ask questions about what you see on the map to push a student's thinking deeper, and invite them to keep working on it.

The same goes for OTAs and rambling writing. If you look at them at all, only mine them for information that helps you support your students' growth. Look for where you can show students how to use these tools even more successfully to drive their own learning. Resist the urge to evaluate any of this work on a rubric as you would with a traditional grading approach. (See more thoughts on rubrics in Chapter 5 as well as how to use the Three Step Meaning Making Process to underpin grading.)

We often emphasize the work we ask of our students with points and grades because we want our students to feel like the work they're doing matters. It's easy to think that the best way to get students to do something is to attach a significant grade to it, and I know it feels like students won't do work unless it matters in the gradebook. Like they won't read unless there's a quiz or a test to hold them accountable. Or they won't write any OTAs unless they know that we'll be looking at every single one and grading it. Or they won't ramble or make a concept map to really figure out what they are thinking unless we score these things on a rubric for a grade.

But even those high stakes assessments that feel like they ensure our students will take the work seriously aren't always so certain. A few years ago, I conducted a small experiment: I gave a multiple-choice test about a book. The resulting scores—well over a B average—suggested that most students likely did the reading. But then I asked them each individually if they had read the book and discovered that far fewer of them had done the reading than the multiple-choice test suggested. Tests and quizzes *don't* ensure that students have read. Significant grades in the gradebook *don't* ensure that students are doing the work authentically and meaningfully.

Our students work for grades when that's what *we* emphasize.

We can reframe why students are doing the work. Our students' meaning making should not be about a polished final product that we can grade on a rubric, so we have a number to put in the gradebook. It is about students producing their *own* insights about what they're reading. Instead of emphasizing evaluation, we can observe what they put together as they build their ideas and listen to conversations they have with each other along the way. The valuable insights we learn about their individual reading processes can help us invite them to keep reading, rambling, and thinking in ways that matter to *them*.

## The Goal Is Independence

It sometimes happens—particularly on quiet mornings when I'm rambling alongside my students, pushing on my ideas about a text, trying to wrangle something neat and clear and organized out of the thoughts swirling in my head—that I feel a growing desire to design the perfect graphic organizer or the right set of questions to make meaning clear and orderly for my students. Maybe you've had this urge, too. It's an instinct that reflects our honest and sincere hope to help our students.

But the moment we sort the chaos for them, we excuse them from doing the most important work. In our efforts to illuminate difficult texts for our students, we stop them from voicing their own ideas, and we fail to communicate confidence in their abilities to make sense of challenging reading.

Instead, we can give students the tools *they* can use to sort the chaos *on their own*.

Remember, stepping aside does not mean that we're completely out of the room. There *is* a place for our expertise as more experienced readers. We can model for our students what the *work* of meaning making looks like. We can write our own OTAs and share them—perhaps on details in the text that we want to be sure they think about. We can ramble alongside students—perhaps on some bigger ideas that we want to invite students to think about. We can share our thoughts as students share theirs and describe how we got to those thoughts, modeling our own reading process. But as only one voice in the room in a varied, ongoing conversation about a shared text, not as the expert all others must defer to. We can be thinking partners who put *students'* process out front, using our expertise to nudge and fill in strategies for them to take their ideas from simple noticings to fuller theories about what a text means.

Here's a quick snapshot of what this work can look like when we step aside and let our students drive their own reading.

I sit down at a table with four students, a book club in my colleague Jaime's class. His students have been practicing OTAs and rambling writing as fodder for the book club conversations they have together in class. The discussion I'm joining is about *My Heart Is a Chainsaw* by Stephen Graham Jones (2022). I've just finished the book myself, and I have so many questions—I'm grateful for the opportunity to talk with some other

readers. We begin by sharing all the places we are confused, and I am relieved to know that I'm not the only reader with significant questions about the main character. We realize that the author *wants* us to be confused, so we start pulling out specific text details that drive that confusion.

One student has been quiet for a few moments while she spins back through the pages. "Here!" she says and reads aloud a paragraph. The air reverberates as silence falls across our table and we all look at each other—we've found our Rosetta Stone. Slowly, we piece together a theory about the main character and begin making sense of the questions that started our discussion.

Our conversation isn't linear. It isn't orderly. There are moments when we all look at each other in desperation, worried that we will never actually figure anything out. One student hasn't even yet finished the book—she half listens to our conversation while she reads the final pages. But by the end of class, I've experienced a most exhilarating conversation with a group of students who met me as equal readers. They dove into the uncertainty and questions that a complex text invites, explored tentative ideas, admitted they weren't sure about things, and persisted in looking back through the words on the page to find answers. Sure, I was *a* teacher sitting there with them, but I was not their actual teacher, and I came to the conversation flummoxed about the book. I needed the group to help *me.*

These students knew how to navigate their confusion with the text because they had practiced simple strategies along the way—tracking what they noticed with OTAs and rambling in writing to connect ideas. And we each used the conversation to grow our own thinking about the text. I walked away with the desire to reread for clues I missed the first time through to see if my emerging theory about the main character holds. The conversation prepped the students as they moved toward a timed essay asking them to clearly articulate some aspects of what they've each figured out about the book.

Being ready for a summative assessment on a book is secondary.

More important is students knowing that they can do the complex, difficult work of reading *on their own.*

There are several reasons why the strategies in this chapter produce student-led learning with students driving. The meaning making starts with what the students think, so every subsequent step builds on that student thinking. Wherever they end up is a place unique to each of them:

their own understanding of a text. These are strategies students can use again and again and again, with any text, no matter how complex. And most importantly, this process keeps us out of the way because it anchors on students' original thinking from the start.

Our students can become readers who drive their own journeys through the mess of meaning making. We can show them how without directing their reading with comprehension questions about what seems most important to us, without holding them accountable with reading quizzes, without feeling like we have to explain a difficult text. We can teach them flexible, powerful strategies that they can use on their own with any text. We can invite them into a process where they choose their own path to meaning.

And perhaps that process will help them to read and make meaning from the most complicated texts they'll ever confront: their own lives.

CHAPTER 3

# INVITE STUDENTS TO DRIVE AS WRITERS

*I found it a huge relief to not have to worry about writing what I thought you wanted to hear. I started to come up with my own ideas again and explore them.*

—anonymous twelfth-grade student

The previous chapter anchors on how the Three Step Meaning Making Process can offer students a road map for growing their own thinking as they read complex texts, starting in a simple, low-stakes place: their own noticings about small details in the text. The same Three Step Meaning Making Process can underpin writing instruction, but what we're teaching students to build with it is different.

I'm sure you're no stranger to the idea of teaching writing as a process: prewriting, feedback, revision, polishing. In my own past as a teacher, I structured writing instruction around those steps in the service of students producing final pieces of writing that I would evaluate on a rubric for a significant grade in the gradebook, which I believed added the gravitas necessary for my students to take the writing process seriously and engage in it authentically.

When we emphasize final products, we teach students that writing is all about having that perfect, final piece of writing, and this produces a misunderstanding of what strong writing actually entails. Authentic writing is not linear. It is not neat. It is not a blank page to a polished piece, one word at a time in consecutive order. But that is what our students may come to believe writing is if we don't immerse them in the actual messiness of writing and show them each how to embrace it as they find their own unique writing process.

## How Can We Invite Students to Drive as Writers?

When my students reflect on their writing, I hope to see words like, "I decided to...." I want them to see they have choices to drive the evolution of their writing. When we become directive in our efforts to simplify what's most difficult about the work of writing, we often end up deciding too much for our students. For example, we may determine a topic for them. Or we may instruct them to structure their writing in a certain way. Or we may ourselves create pairings or small groups for peer feedback. Or we may offer only one mentor text to study. In these ways, we end up taking away students' ability to make choices at key points in the process that will enable them to truly drive on their own.

Instead, we can offer several choice points in our writing instruction. Each opportunity for students to choose helps them to feel ownership over their writing process. We can invite students to decide what they want to write about, how they want to structure their writing, which pieces of writing they want to revise, who might be the just-right reader to give them feedback, which mentor text might show them some specific craft moves to imitate to help them reach their goals with their writing, which mechanical aspects they want to strengthen, or even when a piece of writing is polished enough.

Depending on the needs of a particular student or group of students, the expectations of a required curriculum, or the contours of the school calendar, the range of options at each choice point may need to narrow or might have space to broaden. But there is always room for *some* choice. If we hope to create classroom spaces where students are truly driving as writers, they must have opportunities to make writerly decisions for themselves.

Focusing instruction on the messy, choice-laden process of writing gives students the opportunity to practice—again and again—the actual work of writing. This creates a space for students to grow their ability to drive their own process as writers. Figure 3.1 shows how the Three Step Meaning Making Process can help us to organize writing instruction and ensure we keep it focused on the choice points that invite students to drive their own writing process.

| Meaning-making process step | | Writing strategies to teach | Choice points we can offer students |
| --- | --- | --- | --- |
| ONE: | • Capture your initial thinking about your writing. | Answering the magic question<br>Frequent, small revision tasks<br><br>(every week or every other week) | → what to write about<br>→ what small spot in the writing to revise |
| TWO: | • Get ideas to strengthen your writing. | Mentor text study<br>Reader feedback<br><br>(as often as possible) | → which writing to strengthen<br>→ which mentor text to consult and how to use it<br>→ who might be the just-right reader |
| THREE: | • Decide how you want to finalize your writing. | Cleaning up mechanics<br>Polishing a piece of writing<br><br>(at the end of a unit or term) | → which writing to finalize<br>→ which mechanical issue to focus on<br>→ deciding when the writing is finished |

**Figure 3.1** Three Step Meaning Making Process for Writing

## Model Writing Process by Driving Alongside Writers

There is no better place for us to teach what the actual work of writing looks like than from inside the process ourselves. Writing with students offers important perspective into what it takes to do a particular writing task successfully. We may not have the time to write every single task to completion alongside our students. But even a small bit of writing on a particular task can help us to teach it. When we see the work firsthand from the inside—doing what we ask our learners to do—we inform and enhance our teaching in countless ways.

For example, each year when my sophomores turn their attention to memoir writing, I write some memoir, too. Recently, I wrote about watching my mom navigate her new life in a memory care facility. As I was drafting, I realized that I wasn't actually writing a narrative. It was just a reflective piece, so I developed a narrative frame for my memoir that I could share with students who were also writing more of a reflection with little or no actual narrative in it. I was only able to see this strategy from *inside* the process myself.

IF YOU FIND YOURSELF THINKING...

This feels like a lot of moving pieces for writing instruction — varying topics and writing formats, mentor text study, reader feedback, revision work, proofreading for mechanics — and letting students make their own choices about all of it? Sounds like an invitation for chaos. Wouldn't it just be easier to direct all of my students' work myself to hold it all together?

CONSIDER: Plan with intentional flexibility built into a weekly routine that protects time for students to navigate the messiness of revision.

PLANNER my weekly routine

FOR EXAMPLE...

WEDNESDAY

Maybe every Wednesday you put out the week's writing invitation, give students some time to get started, and then do some quick writing instruction surrounding the different revision strategies you'll see in this chapter.

THURSDAY FRID

Then perhaps students know they'll have time in class on Thursday and Friday to finish writing and complete a small revision task*.

It's important that students do the bulk of this work in class so you can...

observe and interact with your students,

gauge their growth and understanding,

and offer support as they work.

*See chapter 6 for more on weekly routines that support students to drive as writers.

Students will need more instruction and modeling at the start of the year and less and less as time goes on.

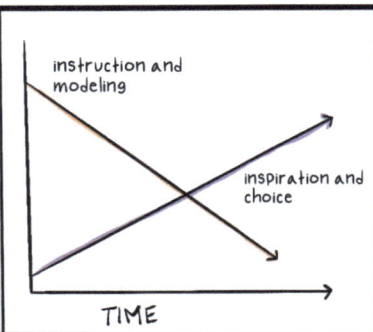

instruction and modeling

inspiration and choice

TIME

If a student knows how to do the work and is confident in driving it, then they will hold together all the pieces of their OWN writing process.

**Figure 3.2** Backseat Driver Warning

Students should witness the fits and starts we have as we write. We should talk through how mentor texts are giving us ideas for revision. We can ask *them* to be our readers and then talk through how their feedback is inspiring our plans for revision. We can share revision strategies that we figure out as we write ourselves.

We can be our students' model for what it actually looks like to drive as writers.

## *Start Small*: Teach Students to Capture Their Initial Thinking About Their Writing

The strategies in this chapter depend on students already having some words on the page. Invite frequent, low-stakes, informal writing. Similar to the original thought annotation (OTA) presented in the last chapter where readers start by noticing small details and capturing their thinking about them in order to grow their own ideas about a text, figuring out their own writing process begins with students' initial, tentative writing that they can then build into something more. Deciding which of that writing they want to work with is a choice point that invites students to feel ownership.

Chapter 6 will offer some ways to think about how to build a weekly routine that includes the volume of writing necessary for writers to grow (and how to think about making a large volume of student writing manageable for the teacher). For the purposes of this chapter, imagine students are turning in a rough piece of writing every week or every other week. It's rough because it's low stakes, ungraded (in a traditional sense—more on this later in this chapter), tentative, exploratory. Students should make sure the piece of writing has a beginning, middle, and end. But other than that, the students can consider it not totally complete yet, a piece of writing that would definitely need more work before they called it done.

### *Invite Students to Answer the Magic Question*

"If you were to keep working on this, what would you focus on?"

This question is magic because it gets students thinking about revision early on, ensuring that all subsequent revision work builds from their *own* ideas. The question is also magic because our students' answers enable us to plan writing instruction anchored on what *they* say they want to improve. We can follow students through their writing work as they drive on their own. For example, if several students say that they would focus on weaving in more evidence from their personal experience, then you might decide to offer a mini lesson on exactly that.

The magic question also emphasizes the choice students have as writers. The "if" reminds students that at some point they will decide *if* they'll keep working on the piece of writing. You might require them to revise, but they will be able to choose the piece of writing. As students answer the magic question, they capture their in-the-moment thinking about a particular piece of writing in case they come back to revise it later.

I include the magic question in the prompts for the writer's memo my students include with every piece of writing they turn in to me, something I have done consistently since I learned about writer's memos in a workshop with the Colorado Writing Project several years ago. The memo prompts ask students to write about what they are most proud of, what was challenging, what their intended audience and purpose was, and—of course—to answer the magic question. Here's a writer's memo from a sophomore, Robin:

> I am so proud of how I wrote my poem and made it rhyme. I got some help from my dad because he used to write poems. I think what was challenging was getting into the zone and writing with my heart and not my brain. My topic was about mothers' love and how it can be tough, my intended audience was teenagers with mother problems, and the genre is a poem that I wrote. I think I would keep adding more imagery.

Writer's memos offer such important insight into students' thinking about their writing. I'm thrilled that a writing task in my class offered Robin and his dad an opportunity to connect over poetry. "Teenagers with mother problems" shows that Robin is thinking carefully about a specific intended audience. His answer to the magic question—to "keep adding more imagery"—gives me feedback that the work we had done together in class studying imagery in the poetry of Hanif Abdurraqib is indeed helping Robin figure out how he wants to drive his own writing. If he does choose to come back later to finalize this piece of writing, he will be able to start with his initial thinking about it, captured in his writer's memo.

### *Invite Frequent, Small Revision Tasks*

I used to only ask students to revise after they had completed a few pieces of writing over several weeks. But I soon realized that if those occasional revision assignments are the only time students practice it, they are not revising enough to build skills to live confidently in the messy writing process space. Now, I include a small revision task with each rough piece of writing students turn in. The tasks are small and quick so students can easily accomplish them.

I fear that in the ways I used to invite it, revision was onerous. My thorough revision tasks required students to address nearly every bit of what they had written. These tedious assignments also left me with multiple stacks of papers that I had to deal with, that took me hours. And I often had to send writing back to students several times to keep working. I was *always* dealing with multiple revisions to review—significant work I created for myself.

That's not to say that I don't ask my students to finalize a piece of writing every so often—maybe two to three times per semester via a less onerous revision invitation (which I'll describe later in this chapter). If I want my students to become skilled and independent at revision, and if I want my students to understand the critical role revision plays in crafting effective writing, they need to be revising regularly.

Revision is a constant part of writing. I can't even tell you how many words I've written on this document that will never see publication. I completely rewrote this chapter based on a realization I had in my classroom one day. There have been several bath-tub epiphanies that have helped me achieve more clarity. Serpentine sentences come out of my head first. I write and then I have to delete as much of it as I can. In *Craft in the Real World*, Matthew Salesses explains that "revision is the craft through which a writer is able to say and shape who they are and what kind of world they live in" (2021, 39). Writing guru Peter Elbow describes revision as "what the words don't yet say, but want to say" (*Writing with Power*, 1998, 145). If students learn what it means to revise, then students learn what the work of writing truly entails.

Making the work of revision as concrete as possible helps students see ways they can approach it. The framework Kelly Gallagher offers in *Write Like This*, RADaR Revision (2011, 206) [see Figure 3.3], can help students clearly identify some possible next steps. Is there something they want to replace or add? Something they want to delete? Something they want to reorder? A simple, concrete framework such as this can help students envision what it means to revise their writing.

| R | A | D and | R |
|---|---|---|---|
| **Replace...**<br>...words that are not specific.<br>...words that are overused.<br>...sentences that are unclear. | **Add...**<br>...new information.<br>...descriptive adjectives and adverbs.<br>...rhetorical or literary devices. | **Delete...**<br>...unrelated ideas.<br>...sentences that sound good but that don't help you achieve your overall purpose.<br>...unwanted repetition.<br>...unnecessary details. | **Reorder...**<br>...to make better sense or to flow better.<br>...so details support main ideas.<br>...to vary the delivery of chronological details. |

**Figure 3.3** RADaR: The Four Steps of Revision
Source: Adapted from Gallagher 2011.

Modeling is key here. Show students what the work of writing looks like in the midst of the messy process of revision. Using one student's writing on the big screen and having them talk through what they're wanting to change can be a great opportunity to model replacing, adding, deleting, and reordering. Modeling this with your own writing can be incredibly powerful, too.

Ask students to revise only one place in every rough piece of writing they turn in to you. Just one place. And they get to decide where. They can point it out to you with a margin comment to explain the change they make with comments like, "I added this repetition because I like the repetition in the poem we read together in class."

Inviting one small revision captures students' initial thinking about a piece of writing. If they do choose to come back to the piece of writing later to polish and finalize it, they will have already started, anchored on what *they* notice and want to improve in their own writing. This invites them to drive their own writing process.

## *Seek Connections*: Teach Students to Get Ideas to Strengthen Their Writing

In the second step of the Three Step Meaning Making Process, students will start to seek connections to build on the ideas they've already had about how to strengthen their writing. There are choice points at this step that can encourage students to build yet more ownership over their own process. For one, they can look back over a few pieces of writing and select one they want to work on more. Other choice points include deciding whether to work on their own to find ideas to revise using a mentor text or if they want to find a just-right reader to give them feedback on their work. Either way, they can start from their answer to the magic question and the small revision task they already did.

This is *very* different from how I used to approach revision. In the past, my students always revised in response to *my* feedback. Now, if I plan to include my feedback in their writing process, it happens *after* they have already revised using the mentor text study and/or reader feedback they already did on their own. Following students as they each drive their own writing process is a powerful vantage point for a teacher. We can study their revision work to figure out what instruction will help them achieve the goals they have for their own writing. We can look for places to nudge them toward curricular expectations. We can mine their revisions for strong examples to share with the whole class. Reading student writing for this purpose—to design instruction that responds to the work they are driving themselves—takes far less time than writing detailed, individualized feedback to every single student. Trusting students to drive saves *us* time and energy.

BACKSEAT DRIVER WARNING
IF YOU FIND YOURSELF THINKING...
My students won't have any idea what to revise in their writing if they don't get my feedback first so I can make suggestions.
CONSIDER:
Asking students to revise BEFORE they get teacher feedback teaches them to be more proactive about figuring out how and what to revise.

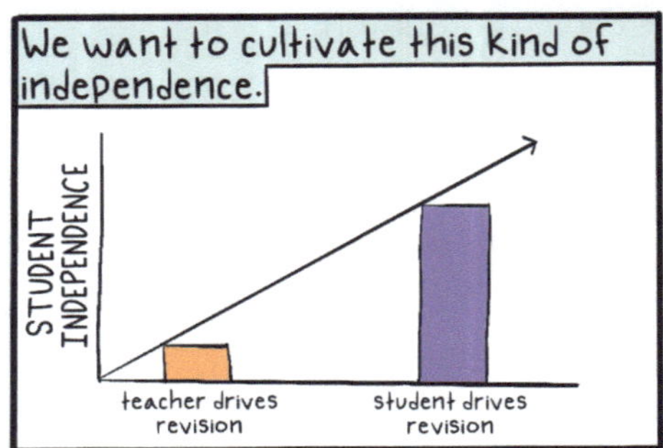
We want to cultivate this kind of independence.
STUDENT INDEPENDENCE
teacher drives revision
student drives revision

And even though they might be attempting to do revision work without our suggestions...
How can I make my writing better?

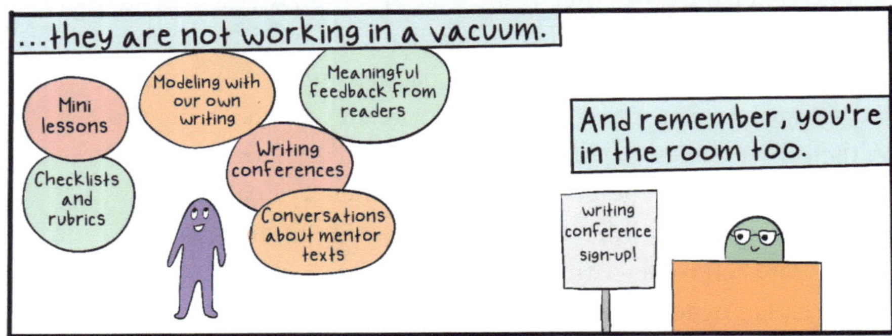
...they are not working in a vacuum.
Mini lessons
Modeling with our own writing
Meaningful feedback from readers
Writing conferences
Checklists and rubrics
Conversations about mentor texts
And remember, you're in the room too.
writing conference sign-up!

As a result, students learn and hone writing process strategies that they can repeat on their own for the rest of their lives.
Independent WRITER!

**Figure 3.4** Backseat Driver Warning

## Using Mentor Texts: An Independent Strategy for Students to Strengthen Their Writing

A few years ago, my cousin asked me to officiate her wedding. I said yes, and then I got a little bit terrified. I had no idea what I would say!

I did, however, know where to start: I needed some models.

I wondered about the common characteristics—how were wedding ceremonies organized? What tone did they strike? What kind of language did they use? How did they begin and end? What were their parts and pieces? I found a few examples on the internet. I read a copy of what a colleague had written for his own wedding.

By using successful models as examples to help answer my questions, I was ready to compose a ceremony just right for my cousin. Later, when another cousin asked me to officiate her wedding, I was ready to go.

The point is that by knowing how to find models and read them like a writer, I was able to figure out a new writing task on my own, which is the skill I hope for my students once they leave my classroom. Teaching students to find models gives us a way to demystify writing: students learn that they can figure out how to approach any writing task on their own.

### Finding Mentor Texts

When we include models of actual, living writing in writing instruction, students see that they are not just producing forms of writing that show up in school and nowhere else. The classroom becomes a place to work on the same types of writing that exist beyond the school's walls.

The curriculum, the task, and/or the group of students all color how you might go about putting together a collection of mentor texts. Consider:

- If students are all working on the same genre at the same time, select a few strong examples of that genre to read and discuss. For example, in an Advanced Placement (AP) Literature class where students need frequent practice of the literary analytic writing they'll do on the AP exam, look at examples of critical reviews of films and books. Think about the ways writers use details from those texts in their writing, how they interject voice into what they write, and how they break formulaic approaches that students often fall back on, like the five-paragraph essay.

- If students are working on the same writing purpose (narrative, informative, or argumentative) at the same time, select examples of a few different genres that could work for that purpose. For example, perhaps a ninth-grade curriculum includes some informative writing about food. Collect some recipes, some descriptions of meals or restaurants, a glossary of food terms, a news article about a restaurant opening, and an explanation about veganism. Students could use these to imagine the different possibilities for their writing, both by topic and by genre.
- If there's a whole-class text that you teach, use it as a shared mentor text. My colleagues and I have done this in a senior class with Krakauer's (1997) *Into the Wild* as a mentor text for journalistic feature writing and with Baca's *A Place to Stand* (2001) as a mentor text for memoir writing. In a sophomore class, we've used Satrapi's (2004) *Persepolis* as a mentor text for memoir writing in the form of comic panels.
- If students have wider choice for purpose and genre, build a collection that they can explore. Use the three main writing purposes—narrative, informative, and argumentative—to organize the collection. List common genres under each purpose. If you make it a hyperdoc, you can link to online collections of particular genres or resources about them—like a link to *Flash Fiction Online* in the narrative section, an online magazine where students can see many examples of flash fiction. Not every genre listed would need to have a hyperlink, but you can add more hyperlinks over time.

You can also engage a class of students in building a mentor text library for a particular writing task. Say a class is spending a few weeks practicing commentaries and then choosing one to revise. Start the library with three commentaries that vary in some way—perhaps by how strongly the writer states their opinion. After reading and discussing all three, invite students to find their own examples, providing a few online publications as a starting point. On a shared document, students can list the mentor texts they find, provide links to them, and write a few words about why they chose the mentor text. When students later choose a mentor text as inspiration for revision, they could use any mentor text on that document, not just the ones you chose for them to begin with.

Inviting students to seek out their own mentor texts is important for cultivating independence as writers. If all of the texts come from the teacher, students don't get experience in finding and evaluating potential models. While they might be able to complete the assignments in our classes with only the models we give them, our lovingly compiled collections won't help them when they need models for writing beyond our classes.

Additionally, when only one person provides models, that individual's perspectives and preferences shape the collection. Instead, we can encourage students to submit pieces of writing that they find worthy, important, or inspirational and share their reasoning with the class, as Chavez suggests in *The Anti-Racist Writing Workshop* (2021). In this way, we make room for differing voices and perspectives, and we communicate trust in students' judgment, which goes a long way toward building confidence in themselves as writers.

### Studying Mentor Texts

When studying mentor texts, we are reading as writers. Any close reading strategies you already teach are useful here. For example, "I noticed..." and "I think..." (sticky note OTAs—see Chapter 2) can be a simple protocol for students to identify something happening in a mentor text and the impact they think it is having. A student might write "I notice a lot of sentence fragments," followed by, "I think this shows the moment is intense." The OTA then becomes a student's own articulation of a possible craft move to try out in their revision.

With any mentor texts your whole class looks at together, focus on teaching students the process: how to notice moves authors make and then how to think about the impact of those moves. It may start with you pointing out some craft moves that *you* notice and then thinking out loud about what you think the impact is. Depending on the needs of your students, you may have to do a lot of this kind of modeling before they are driving this work on their own. That's okay. Take the time to show them how. Just always remember that your goal is to eventually step aside so they can do the thinking without you.

If students start revision work with the initial thinking they already captured about their writing (their answer to the magic question and/or the small revision task they've already done), that thinking can be their primary lens for studying the mentor text. For example, if a student answered the magic question with something like, "I would probably make it a little bit more detailed," they could look for places in a mentor text where an author writes with specific detail, thinking about its impact. If that same student already tried adding a bit more detail via a small revision task, they can seek places in the mentor text that have similar specific detail and see if they can imitate the author's strategies.

When students approach mentor text study with their initial thoughts about their *own* writing, *they* decide how they seek out and use mentor texts. We can support them as they drive this work by introducing them to a variety of "moves" that authors make. Many of my students have found Marchetti and O'Dell's (2015) list of craft moves helpful [Figure 3.5]. Using

| | |
|---|---|
| **Structure Moves** | Focus on how the pieces of the text work together. For instance, does it have strictly or more loosely defined sections? How does it move from one paragraph, or stanza, to the next? Is there a clear beginning and ending? |
| **Ideas and Detail Moves** | Focus on the content of the piece, large and small. For instance, do unexpected details pop up in the writing? Are topics included that you had not previously considered? What do you notice about the content and the ideas brought up by the author? |
| **Sentence Moves** | Focus on the syntax, punctuation, and patterns that create striking sentences. For instance, does the writer use interesting syntax (sentence structure) or repetition that you could mimic? Is there unique punctuation or line breaks? |
| **Word Choice or Tone Moves** | Focus on the specific words and attitude employed by the writer. For instance, does the writer use interesting word combinations? What in the writing signals the attitude of the writer toward the subject? How could it help you sharpen your own attitude in your writing? |

Figure 3.5 Four Kinds of Craft Moves to Study in Mentor Texts
Source: Adapted from Marchetti and O'Dell 2015, 78.

the options in this list, you might invite students to find one craft move from each category. Or you could invite them to zero in on one or two of the categories that best line up with what they already want to work on in the piece. Or you could send the whole class on the hunt for craft moves from one particular category and then look at some together.

Picture one of your students looking across a series of sticky note OTAs, each capturing a craft move *they* noticed in a mentor text *they* chose because it lines up with what *they* said they wanted to work on in a piece of writing. They've got a custom, ready-made, just-for-them (created by them!) list of possible craft moves to explore as they revise. They're building skills they can use to figure out any writing situation for the rest of their lives.

## *Finding Just-Right Readers for Feedback: A Strategy for Students to Work with Others to Strengthen Their Writing*

A thoughtful reader's feedback is a gift to any writer.

When we've built a strong classroom community, there will be many potential thoughtful peer readers in every classroom. Together with your students, you can establish routines and conditions that make turning to each other for reader feedback easy and efficient. Yet, even with the strongest, most welcoming classroom community, there are times when students just don't want to share their writing with their classmates. Perhaps they've taken a risk with a very personal writing topic. Or perhaps they are making the tiniest baby steps in their confidence about their words on the page. We can put students in charge of determining who their readers will be and show them how to direct their readers to give them the feedback they most need.

### Coach Students on How to Find the Just-Right Reader for a Particular Piece of Writing

Peer feedback is a staple of writing classrooms. In the past, I would simply match up students with a classmate and have them read and give each other feedback. But when we determine for students who they'll get feedback from, we take away an important decision they can make for themselves as they are developing more and more ownership in their work.

I tell my students that their just-right reader might be sitting next to them in the classroom, but they can choose anyone in their life (except me!) to give them feedback: peers in other classes, siblings or parents at home, even grandparents working from a distance on a Google Doc. I was thrilled one year when a sophomore told me that she had been a reader for her sister the previous year—when her sister was in my senior class. I remembered the thorough, thoughtful feedback the older sister had received from her chosen reader, and I had no idea that reader was her ninth-grade sister!

What makes for a just-right reader depends on each piece of writing. A student might choose someone who has expertise in the specific type of writing—like we saw in the writer's memo from my student Robin earlier in this chapter. He worked on his poem with his dad because his dad writes poetry. A student might choose someone they feel safe with—like a good friend they know will be kind as they read something that took real courage to put on the page. Or a student might choose someone who has some knowledge about the topic they're writing about—like a family member who can offer more detail to a distant memory for some memoir writing (especially if the student's answer to the magic question indicated that they wanted to add more specific detail). A student's initial thoughts about a piece of writing should drive their selection of a reader for feedback.

For students whose just-right readers are outside of class, some flexibility on due dates can help so they can account for the time needed to get Grandma on the phone for a conversation about a piece of writing. Not only is it wonderful to see students reaching out to the important people in their lives for feedback, it's also heartening to know that in the future, long after they've left our classroom, they will know how to find a reader.

There's always a risk that students may not choose the best reader if they can choose anyone they want from their life. It may seem that limiting potential readers to the students in the room means that you can step in to help them to be the best readers for each other. But think about the potential learning opportunities for students if they choose a reader who is not very helpful: the outcome of that one decision will color their future choices for feedback partners, improving their ability to select the best readers for their writing.

### Teach Students How to Give Their Readers Guidance as They Read

Just because someone is a thoughtful and supportive friend, relative, or peer doesn't mean that they know how to give a writer useful feedback. Teach students how to help their readers give them the feedback they need.

Students are pretty savvy already about what good feedback *isn't*, and that's often a great place to start. Ask your class "Who's got an example of some feedback you got on your writing that wasn't helpful?" and you'll hear things like:

- Just writing "good" without telling me what's good.
- Fixing errors and doing nothing else.
- Telling me how to rewrite it in a way that sounds like them, not me.

From this opening conversation, students are ready to consider better ways to coach their readers toward feedback that could grow their writing.

Start with defining what you mean by "feedback." Offering principles such as these (Zerwin, 2020), can help your students coach their readers:

1. Feedback should help the student grow as a writer; the goal is not only to improve the specific piece of writing.
2. Feedback should reflect—like a mirror—not evaluate.
3. Feedback is a conversation.
4. Feedback should cause thinking.
5. Feedback should tie to a student's own goals for the piece of writing.

I project these on the board and ask students to copy them into their writer's notebooks as I talk through each principle. Inviting students to relate these principles to instances when they've found feedback very helpful (or *not* helpful) can help them to see the kind of feedback they want to direct their readers to provide. Number 5 is a good reminder to go back to their initial thoughts about the piece of writing (their answer to the magic question and the small revision task) to focus their chosen reader on the feedback they most need. Great feedback doesn't just happen by handing someone your writing and asking them what they

- ❑ There is an obvious opinion.
- ❑ Put your thesis where it makes the most sense.
- ❑ Establish the issue early.
  - ❑ Make sure the topic is one that other people may have differing opinions on.
- ❑ Use your own voice.
  - ❑ Sound like you know what you're talking about (helps with your credibility).
  - ❑ Use the right words to say what you want to say.
  - ❑ Be concise.
- ❑ Include some facts, data, or examples to support and validate your opinion.
  - ❑ Explain how those things support/validate your opinion.
- ❑ Provide necessary background information.

**Figure 3.6** Genre Checklist for Commentary Created by a Class of Twelfth Graders

think. Writers have to use their *own* ideas about their writing to drive feedback sessions.

Depending on the particular writing a student is working on, they might also find a rubric or checklist helpful to guide their reader. Students can work together to create checklists that identify the key characteristics of a particular genre of writing like the checklist in Figure 3.6. After they've read and discussed a few examples of a genre, they're ready to list the characteristics those mentor texts share. In only a few minutes, students can talk to each other in small groups about what they think should be on the checklist and then share ideas out to the whole class. Take notes on the board, and once you've got a list, ask the class for their permission to summarize it into a useful checklist to guide their continued work in the genre. A checklist such as this is something that a writer and a reader can look at together, using it to guide their conversation about a piece of writing.

## *Take Action*: Coach Students to Decide How They Want to Finalize Their Writing

The third step of the meaning-making process invites us to make space for students to decide how they want to finalize their writing, which might happen at the end of a unit or at the end of a semester or at some other interval that makes sense (see Chapter 6 for ideas about planning so students can work through the three steps of the Meaning Making Process). No matter when finalizing writing happens, there are important choice points where students can be driving their writing process: cleaning up mechanics and inviting students to polish some writing and decide when it is done.

### *Cleaning Up Mechanics*

Even in the context of my points-free, feedback-focused, no-penalty-for-risks-taken writing classroom, there was an area I had overlooked where I was still exerting power over my students' writing. When my students were finalizing their writing, no comma splice, punctuation error, or sentence fragment got past me and my metaphorical red pen. I pointed out every single error and required my students to keep working until they had fixed them all. I felt good about making sure my students' writing was free of errors and dressed properly for the function it was attending, so no one would look sideways at it for wearing a t-shirt and jeans when everyone else was in formal wear.

The work of college composition teacher and professor Asao Inoue challenged me to think about this differently. He argues that "standards [about writing] are set by those in power. It's a power move. It's how one group colonizes the minds of another" (2020). In my efforts to make sure my students' writing was correct, I was doing exactly this, enforcing standards about mechanical correctness, standards set and held up by a million grammar exercises and generations of teachers filling the margins of students' writing.

When we do this, we tell students that their way of using language is only okay if it's "correct" according to the standard rules of English—with no comma out of line.

Yes, of course there are *rules* about commas. They don't just go into sentences wherever the writer wants a pause. I pride myself on knowing those rules and following them. About commas. About semicolons. About pronouns and antecedents. About complete sentences (except for when I want to use fragments for effect). I love this stuff. But passing on that value of "correctness" to my students by holding them to that standard is not something I choose to do anymore.

Here are three things to do instead:

- First: Ask students to proofread the first piece of writing they are finalizing for your class on their own, identifying the errors they can see and attempting to fix them. Review their proofreading work carefully, making a list of the common errors that they catch and another list of the common errors they don't catch. The lists will show what your students already know and don't know about language, making it possible for you to plan instruction targeted on building their knowledge about mechanics.

- Then: Based on what you see in your students' initial proofreading work and the lists you made, create a document with their common mechanical errors. Include hyperlinks to resources where students can learn more about each issue of mechanics. The next time students are finalizing a piece of writing, invite them to choose one or a few common errors that they want to work on. Ask them to tell you in a writer's memo which mechanical issues they worked on and to point out a few places where they fixed some errors so you can monitor their understanding.
- Also: Talk about (and model) language use in ways that will help students master language more and more. Strong communicators manipulate language intentionally to achieve their goals as communicators. We can teach students to harness the power of language. If you plan time to focus on mechanics as students are finalizing writing (see Chapter 6 for ideas), you'll have space to model your own adventures with mechanics and to invite students to do the same. Just a few minutes can have a big impact, showing students ways to drive language so they can get it to say exactly what they want it to.

We know that the research on teaching mechanics says that it only works when taught in the context of students' writing (Anderson, 2005, 12). I thought I was achieving that when I was making my students fix all of the errors I had marked in their writing. But these strategies—with students driving—are *truly* in the context of students' writing, right in the middle of their process as writers.

### *Polishing a Piece of Writing*

Asao Inoue's argument about the power dynamics in writing instruction (2020) isn't just about mechanics. Our rubrics typically spell out things like where a thesis should go, how a paragraph should be organized, or what should happen in an intro or conclusion. Though I gave up scoring writing on rubrics for grades many years ago, I still had qualities of writing in my head that would help me determine when I could consider a student's piece of writing complete with no more resubmissions of revision work necessary. I would ask a student to keep working until I thought they had learned what the particular piece of writing could teach them. But I was still holding the power. It was *my* decision about whether or not the writing was finished.

Instead, we can offer simple invitations for students to polish their writing, with steps that provide students opportunities to hone their own writing process. Figure 3.7 shows an example, some instructions I recently offered my tenth-grade students to look back over a few weeks' worth of writing and select a potential piece for their end-of-semester writing portfolio.

ONE: Choose something you have written so far for this class.

TWO: Get some reader feedback or find a mentor text to give you ideas for revision.

THREE: Do some significant revision using the reader feedback or mentor text.

FOUR: Write a new memo at the top of your document:

- What is this piece of writing?
- What are you most proud of?
- What did you change as you polished this piece, and how did your reader feedback or your mentor text inspire the revision?
- Do you think the piece of writing is finished? Or what might you focus on if you kept working on this?

**Figure 3.7** Instructions to Polish Up a Potential Portfolio Piece

Here are some anonymous tenth-grade student responses to the writer's memo prompts in Figure 3.7. I present them as a collage to emphasize the many different directions students took their writing, each driving the writing journey that they needed and wanted to take.

What is this piece of writing?

- This piece of writing is a persuasion piece debating which came first, the chicken or the egg.
- This piece of writing expresses my core values and shows how I use them in my life.
- This piece of writing is arguing that my favorite artist should drop a new album.
- This piece of writing was about which of the United Nations sustainable development goals I find most important.
- This writing is my opinion of how Antigone should have buried her brother and how she should have gotten away with it.

What are you most proud of?

- I am proud of how I took an argument and backed it up with facts. I feel that this makes the argument more elevated.
- I am proud of how I worked and the way I got my writing on the paper.
- I am really proud of the story I told. I really like how I connected my core values and explained how they impact my life.
- I am most proud of how complete the argument is after adding the revisions.

What did you change as you polished this piece, and how did your reader feedback or mentor text inspire the revision?

- My classmate added some comments telling me to add little stories about my experiences. That really helped me because I would've never done those revisions and from now on I will try to include those in future pieces of writing.
- I added description and italic dialogue which I was inspired to do from my mentor text.
- After my reader feedback, I changed simple things such as grammar and spelling. I swapped out words and took away parts of the sentence that I didn't need. I also went back and added more evidence to back up my claim. My reader feedback was quite helpful because it still let me have freedom as a writer.
- I used a technique from my mentor text of questions and answers to create a story.
- The revisions I did were based on my classmate's analysis that I needed to add more depth and detail to the writing. I also got inspiration from our argument checklist, because I originally didn't have any point of view on the other side of the argument.
- The reader feedback I got was that the writing didn't really have a targeted audience, so I decided to add a paragraph orientated towards lawmakers.
- My mom helped me with the revisions and I chose to add details of what my core values are.

Do you think the piece of writing is finished? Or what might you focus on if you kept working on this?

- If I kept working on this, I would try to make it funnier.
- Now that I read the essay all together with my new beginning it sounds a lot better. I am pretty happy with this piece and haven't found anything more I need to fix.
- If I were to keep working on this, I would continue talking about my stories as a child.
- If I were to keep working on this I would try to find more ways that Antigone could have gone about her plan.

As these students articulate the varied decisions they made along their writing journeys, I hope you see signs of their growing ownership, places where they are driving as writers. Our students' final, polished pieces of writing are far less important than the learning they can do while immersed in discovering their own writing processes. We can help focus students on the steps they take through the messy space that is authentic writing, thereby setting them up to build the confidence they need to drive any writing task they encounter in their lives beyond our classrooms.

## A Quick Word About (Not) Grading and Assessment

Feedback and evaluation are not the same thing. Feedback responds to a writer, human-to-human, and has potential to grow the writer. Evaluation puts writing up against an established set of standards and offers a judgment on it: A/B/C/D/F, partially proficient/proficient/advanced, 15 points out of 20. It doesn't matter what form the evaluation takes; it ranks students' writing and communicates that some of it is less than and some of it is more than. Evaluation—especially if it is constant and high stakes—has potential to harm writers.

Failure is a natural part of the writing process: we revise because our words are not quite meeting our intentions for them. If writers are under constant, high-stakes evaluation, failure is risky because it leads to low scores or grades or points. If we are serious about teaching students what the work of writing actually looks like, constant evaluative grading gets in the way. It makes writing in school a mere act of compliance.

Putting student writers in the driver's seat of their writing process can change this paradigm. As Liz Prather explains so eloquently: "Because they write from ownership and not from compliance, writing becomes a pronouncement of self onto the world, a reward larger than any grade on a report card. Developing a writing identity helps to shift writing away from a teacher-directed activity to a student-pursued one that lasts a lifetime" (2022, 11).

The specific strategies that this chapter describes are the same processes that writers employ: reflection, mentor text study, reader feedback. Newkirk reminds us that, "Quality is a byproduct of these writerly processes. These *habits* are the true takeaway of a writing course—and they should be the focus of a writing course, and of assessment" (2021, 109).

Students' answers to the magic question, their small revision tasks, the notes we see in the margins of their writing from their chosen readers, their memos describing what they attempted in revision—these are all valuable assessment data sources. We can see how our students are thinking, what makes sense to them and what doesn't, where they're growing and where they're struggling. We can use these data sources to figure out how to better engage student writers as we move through the school year.

If we invite students into their own, authentic process as writers, they will grow. So rather than evaluating student writing for a grade, "grade" their process. Did they go through all the steps? Did they reflect authentically? Call it complete. (See Chapter 5 for ideas on how to use descriptive—rather than evaluative—rubrics to support this type of grading.)

## The Goal Is Independence

Allie didn't see herself as a writer at the start of her sophomore year. She wrote to me: "there hasn't been a specific moment where I have felt like writing was something that was meant for me. Writing has never been my strongest quality."

By November, you can see in her writer's memo that she was using the strategies this chapter outlines and sounding a bit more like a writer:

> Some inspiration I used from a mentor text was Doc Z's Antigone argument. I decided to highlight my thesis in yellow like Doc Z

> highlighted hers so that I could easily go back and identify my thesis to use for the rest of my essay. It helped to see her direct quotes from the text and it inspired me to put at least one in each paragraph. Mainly, I revised with the "A" from RADaR, and I added a bunch of new sentences and words to try and help make the sentences make more sense and have a deeper meaning than what they originally had. If I were to keep working on this I would definitely add some more direct quotes from the text to make my evidence better and make it more persuasive.

In December, Allie's reflections revealed that she wanted to take more ownership of her writing:

> In the past I would always just quickly write my pieces and turn them in and leave the first round of editing up to the teacher. I realized this year after writing my writer's memos that it is extremely important for me to realize some of the things I need to fix, without a teacher's help. I need to be able to recognize these things on my own.

And by February, a writer's memo on a video essay Allie wrote shows some confidence emerging:

> I am most proud of my script because I think it is very informative and can hopefully convince people of how bad plastic is for marine animals, and I think I did a good job with that. The thing that was most challenging was trying to find visuals to go along with what I was saying, I feel like at times the "video" aspect of the video essay is what was the hardest for me. If I were to keep working on this I think I might try to add more fitting backgrounds to what I was talking about so maybe I could make some more informational visuals to further persuade my audience to feel the way I do.

Allie is confident that the words she wrote for her script were persuasive and impactful, and she is able to identify where she knows she could improve her work. Allie is gaining independence as a writer.

The strategies presented in this chapter cultivate student-led learning by starting first with what students want to work on, thereby setting a direction for all their subsequent revision work to grow from that initial, student-driven start. In this way, writers will travel a journey that they plan out themselves, choosing great writing to help them imagine possibilities for their own work and finding just the right readers for feedback. These are strategies students can use again and again, for any writing situation. Our role is to follow them with instruction that supports the writing work they articulate for themselves and to write alongside them, so we can teach from inside of the process showing them what the real work of writing looks like.

In the end, this work isn't just about helping students to be better writers. It's about helping them listen to, trust, and refine their own ideas. It's about helping them to use their voices with conviction—both in our classrooms and into their futures.

CHAPTER 4

# INVITE STUDENTS TO DRIVE THE CONVERSATION IN THE CLASSROOM

"What colors are tied to our emotions?"

This is a question posed by a ninth-grade book club reading *The Astonishing Color of After* by Emily X.R. Pan. After reading and completing a few original thought annotations (OTAs, see Chapter 2) about the initial pages of the book, the group noticed they had all made notes about how the characters were checking in on each other's emotions via asking what color their emotions were.

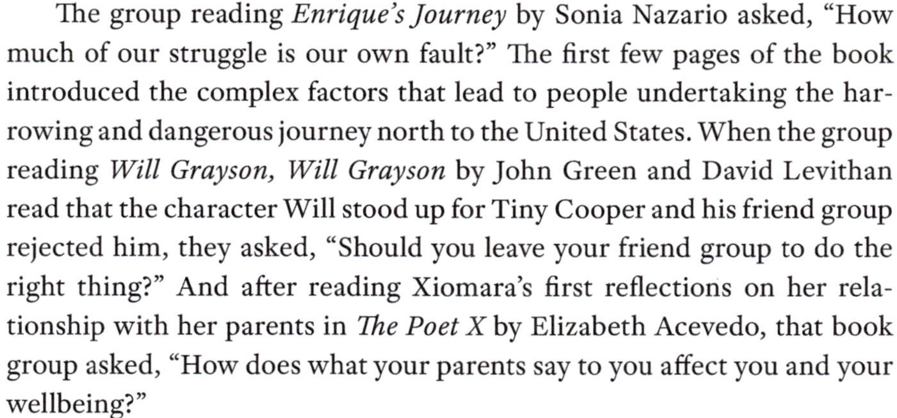

The group reading *Enrique's Journey* by Sonia Nazario asked, "How much of our struggle is our own fault?" The first few pages of the book introduced the complex factors that lead to people undertaking the harrowing and dangerous journey north to the United States. When the group reading *Will Grayson, Will Grayson* by John Green and David Levithan read that the character Will stood up for Tiny Cooper and his friend group rejected him, they asked, "Should you leave your friend group to do the right thing?" And after reading Xiomara's first reflections on her relationship with her parents in *The Poet X* by Elizabeth Acevedo, that book group asked, "How does what your parents say to you affect you and your wellbeing?"

Students posed these questions during the first day of a four-week-long book club unit that would also invite them to practice argumentative and informative writing. The idea was for the book club study to inspire thinking about human life that they could then explore each week in their writing. To provide the opportunity for students to work on the course learning goals about discussion, I planned time for some whole-class conversation each week, which was complicated because students were reading separate texts in book clubs. So we focused on using specific moments from their books to identify some questions about human life everyone could chew on together.

My invitation to students during their very first twenty minutes of silent reading with their book club books was to write at least one OTA on something a character says, thinks, or does that they have some thoughts about. To start conversation in their first book club meetings, they shared what they each captured in those OTAs and selected one sentence from the book that the whole group agreed was worth thinking about more. They used that sentence as the basis of an open-ended question about people in general.

I asked each book club to choose one or more people from their group to join a fishbowl discussion. The book club representative(s) read the sentence the group found in their book, explained its context a bit, and then posed the group's open-ended question. Then conversation opened up for students to take it wherever they wanted to. The listeners on the outside used sticky notes to capture major topics covered and questions posed—sticky notes that they put on the white board after the conversation. This freed me up to just listen and step in where needed to help students make space for each other's voices and ideas.

In their twenty-five-minute conversation about only the first few pages of their book club books, my students explored the following topics: how color ties to emotion, love, what makes us shy or lonely, crisis, whether or not parents should have a strong impact on your future, LGBTQIA+ identity struggles, mental health, being shy and not socializing with others, how life is difficult, struggle, isolation, social anxiety and how it keeps people from interacting with others, difficult decisions, parental influence, global culture, family, why people want to immigrate, figuring out your future, language, and layers of meaning. This list of topics was a rich starting point for the writing they would do that week. Because the conversation anchored on the topics and ideas that *they* pulled from their book club books, the writing that followed grew from life topics that mattered to them, that they chose, that they already talked about together.

Using the Three Step Meaning Making Process to structure talk in the classroom makes a powerful bridge between student talk and the reading strategies in Chapter 2 and between student talk and the writing strategies in Chapter 3. Because the same Three Step Meaning Making Process can underpin how we structure talk in our classrooms, we can use conversations intentionally to support students as they drive their work as readers and writers.

## How Can We Invite Students to Drive Talk in the Classroom?

Here's how three steps of the Meaning Making Process looked with my ninth graders in the opening of this chapter:

1. ***Start small.*** Read and note OTAs about the first several pages of your book club book.
2. ***Seek connections.*** Talk about your OTAs with your book club to identify a key sentence from the reading and come up with a question to offer the class for conversation.
3. ***Take action.*** Pose open-ended discussion questions to the whole class and see where the conversation goes.

This three-step process is similar to a classic method: "Think-Pair-Share," developed by Frank Lyman and his colleagues in 1981. But here we are very intentional about placing students firmly in the driver's seat. The first step, *start small,* gives learners space to think *for themselves* about something that matters to them. It could be a sentence in a text or something they notice in their own writing, depending on the focus of the conversation.

The next step, *seek connections,* invites interactions with a classmate (or a few) to build ideas. Turn and talk with your shoulder buddy. Share at your table. Walk around the room and find two other people to talk with who are wearing similar shoes. However we do it, the point here is to invite students to take the ideas that surfaced when they were thinking on their own and move out into a small, safe space with one or two or three other humans where they can start to see connections and build upon each other's ideas. The third step, *take action,* invites students to take the bigger ideas forming based on connecting their ideas with others and put them out into the wider classroom space. The whole group can explore what they think a shared text means overall or consider what a classmate could do while revising a piece of writing or reflect on whatever it is that the class is chewing on together. Because the first step, *start small*, relies on what learners are thinking and wondering about on their own, once the class gets through the second step and into the third, the big ideas they are wrestling with together are *their* big ideas, not ours.

The process might look a bit different depending on the purpose of the conversation at hand, but the same three steps can be the foundation for conversations that *students* drive. The rest of this chapter invites you to imagine the various opportunities this one powerful strategy presents as we teach students how conversations help them to do the following:

- work as a group to determine meaning from a shared text,
- work on writing together,
- continuously reflect about the day-to-day work of the classroom.

Whether through formalized talk invitations—like whole-class discussions—or the ongoing informal conversations of a classroom community, we can show students how to leverage talking with each other to work through their thinking [Figure 4.1].

| **Meaning-making process step** | **Talk strategies to teach to support students' reading, writing, and day-to-day work** | **Choice points** |
|---|---|---|
| **ONE:** | • conversation prep tasks<br>• selecting OTAs or ideas from rambling thoughts to share with classmates | ➔ what seems important to talk about with classmates |
| **TWO:** | • small group conversation as a bridge to more formal whole-class discussion<br>• share work with classmates in small groups | ➔ what to talk about<br>➔ who to talk with |
| **THREE:** | • using whole-class conversation to develop and hone thinking together<br>• sharing work with the whole class<br>• reflecting on and refining whole-class conversations | ➔ what to talk about<br>➔ how to participate (speak, listen, offer writing for whole-class workshop?)<br>➔ which ideas to capture in note taking for possible future use |

Figure 4.1 Three Step Meaning Making Process for Classroom Talk

## Teach Students to Talk with Each Other to Determine Meaning from a Shared Text

There are umpteen ways to structure a formal conversation in a class. Harkness Table conversations and Socratic Seminars are two specific strategies I use frequently. They are both *student*-centered discussions where students talk with each other, using a shared conversation space to work out the meaning of a complex text together (Ebarvia, 2024; Filkins, 2023). In these text-centered conversations, students drive and the teacher listens, facilitating only to make space for all voices and to help them push their thinking. Teachers can start the conversation with an opening question or invite students to do the same. It's a discussion space students can enter together. I sometimes prepare a handful of open-ended questions that I hope will launch a good conversation. Sometimes all I do is help the students make the conversation table in the middle of the room and invite them to sit at it and start talking with each other. Either way, students usually take it in a direction well beyond what I may have anticipated.

These kinds of whole-class conversations follow the Three Step Meaning Making Process and draw on the reading strategies students may already be using to drive their reading work in the classroom. The first step invites them to *start small* as they gather their ideas for the upcoming discussion via their OTAs, rambling thoughts, or some other individual task. The conversation itself is the *take action* step, a space where students work collectively to determine a text's meaning. I've found that adding in the second step—*seek connections*—between the initial individual task and the actual whole-class conversation boosts participation and engagement because students can connect with others' ideas and test out their own in smaller groups before they offer their ideas to the wider discussion space. I usually enact the connection step with something like, "While I come around the room to check for your preparation task, share with your table your favorite idea and talk together about what you hope today's conversation will explore." I invite students to write down for themselves the best ideas that come up, so they've got something in front of them to refer to once they are actually sitting at the conversation table.

My whole-class conversations are usually opt-in affairs. We squish together a few tables in the middle of the room to make a big conference table, and students who want to talk in the conversation take a seat at the table. For students who would rather listen, I always include a simple listening task to encourage optimal engagement. Ideally the listening task is something that records notes on the conversation like the listening task in the opening anecdote for this chapter or a shared backchannel document projected on the big screen, where those who have opted to listen can capture the big ideas the conversation explores. Sometimes I ask each small group (from step two, *seek connections*) to send at least one person to the larger conversation table to ensure that the whole-class conversation benefits from the work of the smaller step two conversations. Sometimes I ask for a certain number of students at the table, like a third or half of the class. But I don't always do this. Even the smallest groups I've ended up with—only five or so students choosing to sit at the conference table—have been such successful, engaged, conversations that I've regretted having to stop as the class period ends. They remind me of the conversations my dad used to love to stoke around the dinner table!

If I notice a class member who initially chose to listen to the conversation becoming a bit animated, unable to keep from chiming in to the discussion, I invite them to just wheel their chair up to the conference table and join the conversation. After all, we might as well use those wheels on their chairs.

Think carefully about the placement of a whole-class conversation to best support students in their reading work. Will the conversation be the final, step three, *take action*, thing you'll do with the text? Or will it be a space to prepare students for some other culminating task? Sometimes I've scheduled whole-class conversations in the class period before students are to do a final timed essay over a text, so they can use thoughts gathered during the conversation to hone their ideas about the text in preparation for the essay. Or I've asked students to draft a rough concept map about the text as their individual preparation task and then finalize it based on the conversation that unfolds. Or—like in the ninth-grade class from the opening anecdote of this chapter—I've scheduled conversations each week to keep ideas for weekly writing constantly percolating. (Chapter 6 will explore different weekly structures anchored on the Three Step Meaning Making Process.)

Though formal structures like Socratic Seminars and Harkness Table discussions offer a powerful scaffold for students to begin talking and thinking on their own, they are structures essentially set up by teachers. Remember to keep *students* in the driver's seat of these conversations. Toward that, they should always decide *what* to talk about. If we plan time for steps one and two of the meaning-making process before we invite whole-class conversation, they'll be ready to drive that whole-class conversation with their own ideas.

If we always reserve a few minutes after a whole-class conversation for some reflection on how the conversation went, we can co-create the classroom conversation space *with* our students. Ask, "What did you notice about today's conversation? What went well? What could we improve?" The short reflective conversations that follow invite students to imagine creative ways to make the whole-class conversations truly theirs.

| **Start Small step: things to invite students to do individually to prepare for conversation** | **Seek Connections step: things to invite pairs or small groups to do together to prepare for conversation** | **Take Action step: ways for the whole class to use talk together to build meaning about texts** |
|---|---|---|
| Do 1 to 3 **OTAs** (see Chapter 2) on the text (or select your favorite 1 to 3 from previous ones): what do you think would be interesting to talk about? | Select the three sticky note noticings from your group that you think the whole class should consider and be ready to explain why. | Have each group put their findings on a shared google doc, or on the white board, or on a google slide, or pick a representative to share with the whole class. Look for connections, contradictions, and/or common themes to discuss. |
| **Text rendering:** what's the most important paragraph, sentence, and word in a range of text? Why? ("Text Rendering Experience") | Come to consensus in a small group on the most important paragraph, sentence, and word. | |
| TQE: what are your **thoughts**, lingering **questions**, and **epiphanies** about the text? (Thompson, 2018) | Narrow it down to the two top thoughts, lingering questions, or epiphanies in a small group. | |
| What are the **most important** [moments in a character's development / instances of figurative language / symbols / bits of dialogue / plot moments / data presented to support the author's ideas, etc...]? | Come to a consensus as a small group on the most important _____. | |
| Go through your **rambling thoughts** (see Chapter 2) and underline your favorite idea. | Share your favorite idea with a small group and choose one to share with the class. | |

**Figure 4.2** Additional Ideas for Classroom Talk to Support Reading Using the Three Step Meaning Making Process

Successful classroom talk that supports readers as they build their ideas about texts does not always need to be a formal class conversation like a Socratic Seminar or Harkness Table discussion. Figure 4.2 helps to imagine more ways to use the Three Step Meaning Making Process on the fly for informal conversations in class that support students' reading. Need something for students to do while you're taking attendance? Choose a *start small* invitation for them to work on for the first few minutes of class. Got fifteen minutes blocked off for some quick conversation about a shared text? Do three minutes of a *start small* task followed by three minutes of a *seek connections* task; then invite as many groups as time allows to share out what they talked about. Lesson plan didn't require as much time as you thought it would? *Start small*: what ideas most resonated for you today? *Seek connections*: share your thinking with your group. *Take action*: let's hear it! What's resonating? (And if you only get through the first one or two steps—that's okay!) Want to start class by taking five minutes to connect to what they discussed the day before? *Start small*: what did we work on yesterday? (one minute). *Seek connections*: tell your group what you remember (one minute). *Take action*: choose a representative to share with the class (three minutes).

If we use the Three Step Meaning Making Process to structure our students' conversations about the texts they are reading, classroom talk can support students' *own* meaning making.

## Teach Students to Talk with Each Other About Their Writing

In the student-driven writing strategies described in Chapter 3, talk about writing is prominent in step two where students seek feedback from readers to improve their writing. But conversation about writing can infuse all steps of the meaning-making process, thereby supporting writers as they each drive their own process.

I dream of a classroom where students constantly turn to each other to talk about their writing without needing an invitation from me to do so. I would hear discussions naturally pop up between students like, "Hey, I worked on my intro—can you take a quick look at it?" or "I totally changed my topic! Here's what happened...." The reality, though, is that our students may not know how to talk to each other about their writing or feel confidence in doing so. We can teach them and provide ample opportunities to practice. There are two high-impact strategies I turn to time and again to teach students how to talk about writing together: modeling conversation between two writers and a whole-class workshop on one person's piece of writing.

### *Modeling Writing Conversations Between Two Writers*

It's possible that students have never really experienced helpful conversation with someone else about a piece of writing, so they may struggle to even imagine what it looks and sounds like. When I get the sense that my students are not quite getting in the mindset for effective conversations about writing, I'll invite a colleague into my classroom for a few minutes to talk with me about a piece of *my* writing. This takes a bit of preparation: my colleague will need to read my writing ahead of time, and it works best if my students have already read the piece of writing my colleague and I will talk about. But this is a great opportunity to both model what talk about writing looks like and step out of the conversation periodically as a commentator to explain to students what is going on in my thinking during the conversation.

The goal is to make the conversation seem as natural as possible—not always easy when it's happening with a class of writers observing. I'll start by thanking my colleague for reading my draft and for taking the time to talk with me. Then I'll lead with what I hope my colleague can help me to think about. With an aside to my students, I explain that I used our Three Step Meaning Making Process to know what to ask my colleague to focus on. I had to first think on my own, *starting small* with the individual areas of my writing that I wasn't quite happy with yet. Then I had to look across those, *seeking connections* in order to determine the most important things I wanted help with. Then I was ready to *take action* to focus my colleague's thinking in our conversation.

Once my colleague starts responding to my specific request for feedback, I listen and take notes in my notebook (with an aside here and there to tell students what I'm writing down and why). As we chat, I respond with clarifying questions, additional explorations about where my intentions seemed to fall short, or perhaps appeals for ideas about how I might revise, depending on where the conversation goes.

After ten minutes or so of talking with my colleague, I might turn to my students and ask them, based on what they've heard, what my next steps could be. If they've got ideas right away, they can just start telling me. If they are reluctant to share right away, some individual think time followed by brief talk with a neighbor often gets ideas brewing for them to share out to the whole class. I always write their suggestions down (whether I end up using them or not) to model keeping notes to come back to later and show students that I value their ideas.

At the end of the conversation, I model a sincere thank you to my colleague for the conversation as well as an articulation of what I think I'll do next with the piece of writing. In this way, I'm showing students how the writer drives the conversation by starting it and ending it and how the writer shows the reader that they've listened carefully, considering exactly how the reader's feedback has impacted their thinking.

Modeling a conversation about writing can be helpful to students before they seek feedback from a reader themselves, and it can be especially helpful before a class first embarks on a whole-class workshop of one person's writing. It gives them an experience to fall back on as they imagine how they themselves might talk in the workshop, what kinds of things they might say to the writer, how the writer might respond, and so on. And the asides I offer to let them in on what the writer is thinking during the conversation help them to imagine what it would be like to be in conversation with others about their own writing.

Showing writers exactly what it looks and sounds like to talk about writing supports them as they talk with others at all steps of the Meaning Making Process. Writers in step one can talk with each other as they *start small*, thinking aloud to each other as they notice the places in their own writing they might want to improve. Writers in step two can talk to each other to *seek connections* as they ask for and offer feedback or even as they talk over their thinking about how a mentor text inspires possible routes for revision. Writers in step three can talk to each other as they think through how they'll *take action* to finalize their writing. We can model such conversations for them so they can envision what it means to talk about writing at each step in the process.

### *Whole-Class Workshopping a Single Piece of Writing*

Another powerful way to show students what it means to talk about writing—and give them a place to practice it together—is a whole-class workshop on one person's writing. There are various ways to go about it, but the essence of it is that the whole group reads something one individual has written and then offers feedback to that person in a whole-class conversation.

It's scary to share writing with others—no matter how accomplished or experienced you are as a writer. That fear is why it's absolutely critical that we anchor whole-class workshops on what grows the writer over what serves the readers. Both *Craft in the Real World: Rethinking Fiction Writing and Workshopping* by Matthew Salesses (2021) and *The Anti-Racist Writing Workshop: How to Decolonize the Creative Classroom* by Felicia Rose Chavez (2021) challenge the traditional approach to a writing workshop that you may have experienced yourself in a college writing class. I remember I had to bring in photocopies of my draft to distribute to the class, wait for them to read it and write all over it, then listen passively as they talked about it, unable to respond even if they missed something critical about my writing that sent them down a conversation path that wasn't helping me at all. Salesses explains that the traditional approach to workshopping only works if all people in the room have the same or similar cultural background. If the writer is of a different background from the readers—and is silenced by the traditional workshop protocol—the readers don't have access to the cultural knowledge they might be missing to fully understand the writer's work. If the writer is of a background typically marginalized by society, such a workshop conversation can hurt that writer by perpetuating oppressive societal structures. A traditional workshop conversation can become a hostile space that fails to see writers and their work fully.

Instead, we can use workshopping protocols that put the writer solidly in control of every step. This not only creates a safer conversation space for the writer, but it ensures that the teacher remains on the side, leaving space for the writer to leverage the conversation for personal growth. Here's Chavez's protocol (Chapters 6–7 and pages 190–1), summarized with some parenthetical notes to point out where the Three Step Meaning

Making Process helps us to think about how this one classroom strategy works for student-led writing *and* student-led classroom talk:

1) The writer meets with the teacher ahead of time for a pre-workshop conference to discuss how they want to facilitate the workshop conversation. Prior to this meeting with the instructor, the student examines their writing to determine the individual pieces they want to improve (*start small*). In the meeting, the student uses the instructor as a sounding board to determine the most important areas for improvement (*seek connections*). The student then crafts a plan for how they will facilitate the workshop conversation, meaning what exactly they'll ask classmates to focus on (*take action*).
2) The writer reads their own writing aloud to the class, so it is *their* voice as a writer who puts the words into the classroom space.
3) The writer offers questions to guide the conversation before the readers respond, launching the conversation based on the help they need to move forward with their writing.
4) After listening to the writer, classmates reflect for a few moments silently about the feedback they might offer the writer, maybe even write a few thoughts on a sticky note (*start small*). They can then turn to neighbors to discuss their initial ideas (*seek connections*) before they start offering feedback aloud to the writer (*take action*).
5) After the conversation, the writer reflects on the feedback received to determine what is most useful to them considering their goals for the piece of writing (*start small*).
6) The writer meets with the teacher for a post-workshop conference (*seek connections*) where they explain which feedback they'll act on as they revise.
7) The writer revises using the feedback received in the whole-class workshop (*take action*).

Chavez makes the point that each step does more than putting the writer out front, in charge of the workshop conversation. This protocol also protects the teacher's time. The teacher need not read the writing ahead of time—the student will read it aloud to the whole class. The teacher need not prepare for the workshop conversation—the student's own guiding questions will structure the conversation. The teacher need not mark up

the student's draft—the student will be listening and taking notes on the feedback that surfaces during the class conversation. The teacher need not suggest to the student what they should do in revision—the student is determining that on their own. The teacher role takes no prep work and no work outside of class, only an availability to act as a sounding board during the pre- and post-workshop student conferences and clear, focused energy as the workshop conversation unfolds.

I suggest we could step aside even a bit more here. Once students understand both what it means to drive the revision process (Chapter 3) and what it means to use the Three Step Meaning Making Process to structure a conversation, the pre- and post-workshop conferences could happen with a student's table group as the sounding board, rather than the teacher.

In a typical secondary language arts class, it's likely not feasible to run many class sessions as feedback workshops, nor is it necessary for every single student to have their writing workshopped by the whole class. Of course, a whole-class workshop conversation's goal is *always* to help the writer whose work is the focus of the discussion. But there's a secondary and just as important goal: to teach the students how to talk about writing with each other. There may only be enough class time for a half- to full-class-period workshop conversation on one student's writing once every other week or once a month or so. But every day that students are sitting next to each other in class and looking at writing is an opportunity for them to talk to each other about writing. With repeated whole-class emphasis on what both the writer and readers do when talking about a piece of writing, students can then use those strategies on their own, even without direction from the teacher.

## Teach Students to Talk with Each Other to Reflect on the Day-to-Day Work of the Classroom

Though talking about shared texts and about students' writing certainly makes up the bulk of conversation in a language arts classroom, there are many other opportunities to invite student talk. One of my past assistant principals, Sarah DiGiacomo, often reminded us that the ones who are talking are doing the learning. It's a reminder that yes, there are times when the teacher needs to be talking, but we should be mindful to avoid

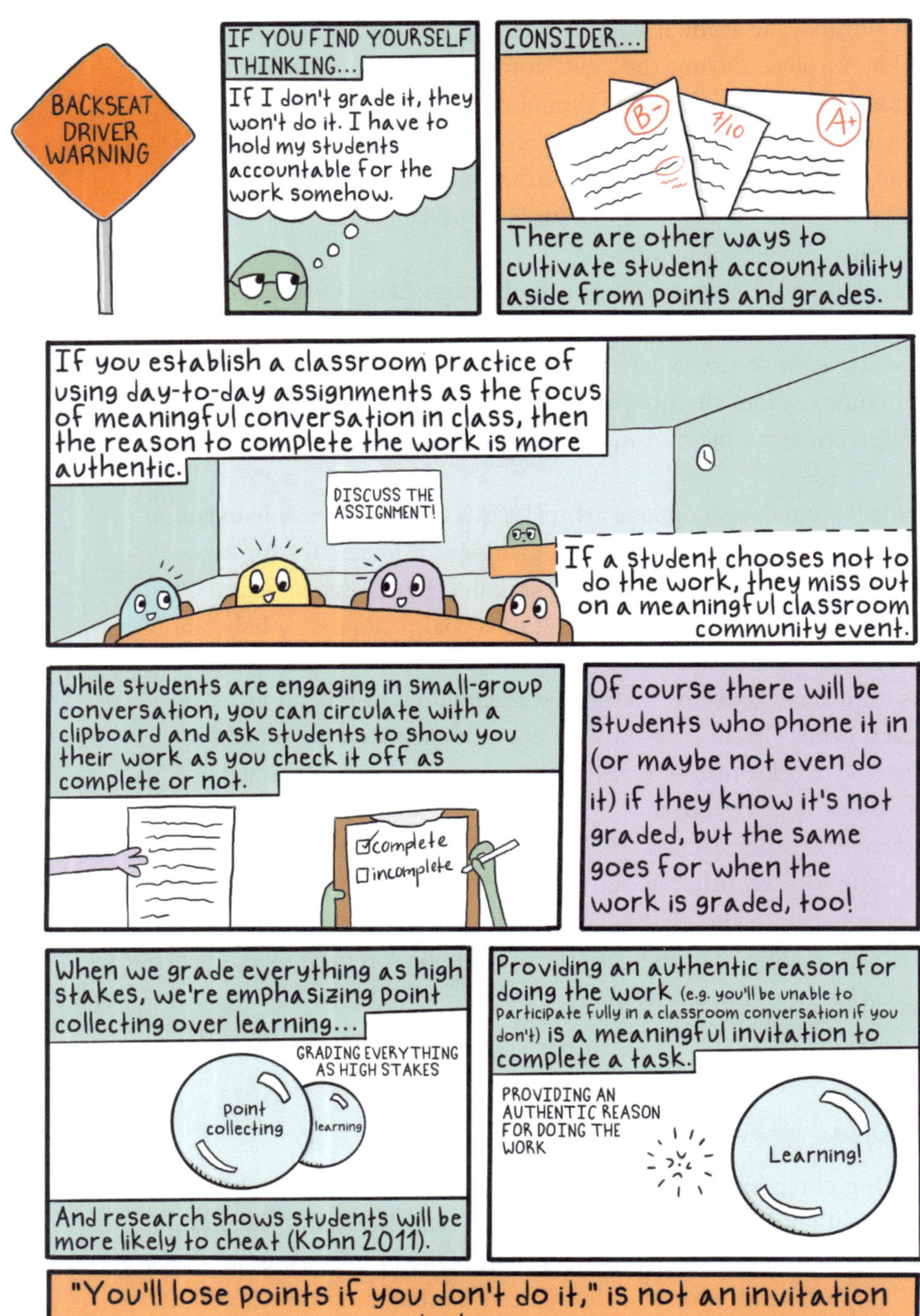


**Figure 4.3** Backseat Driver Warning

talking so much that our voices take up important space where our students could be leading conversations with each other to build their own understanding.

Where can you create space for more talk?

For a start, you can review any kind of classroom task via the Three Step Meaning Making Process, whether the work at hand involves a reading comprehension check, practice on the mechanics and conventions of writing, or preparing for a presentation. The *start small* step is doing the work. The *seek connections* step is comparing it with a classmate or small group. The *take action* step is reporting the work out to the class, maybe with each table group taking the lead on one item in the task. As they compare their work with each other and then determine what to share out with the class, learners are talking with each other about the content, thereby engaging with it much more actively than they would be if you simply talked through the work yourself or graded it on your own and handed it back to them. Yes, conversation often takes precious class time, but if it helps the students learn the material more solidly, it's worth it. Not only does it place learners firmly in control, but this kind of classroom talk can also free up *your* time beyond class. Students *can* get the support and feedback they need on routine classwork via talking about it with their classmates. We don't have to pore over every single task we ask students to complete.

## A Quick Word About (Not) Grading and Assessment

I've seen complex diagrams of Socratic Seminars where a teacher has tracked each student's contributions, all for the purpose of determining a grade for the gradebook. I've seen grading policies on whole-class workshops that spell out how many times a student has to say something to get an A or a B or a C. If our purpose during class conversation is to collect enough data to determine a grade for each student, then that puts us into an evaluative stance during the discussion. And from that perspective, we just can't collect the data that is most important for us to gather.

Instead, we can use this valuable time to figure out who our students are as readers and writers based on what they are saying (or not saying). To observe the dynamics of the conversation so we can monitor how the classroom community is growing (or not growing). To track the ideas that are surfacing (or not surfacing) so we can plan our next instructional steps. We can't do any of that if we're counting students' responses or noting if they quote the text or evaluating the quality of their feedback contributions for the purpose of a grade.

We'll take a closer look at grading in the next chapter. For now, take time to listen as your students talk to each other. Observe the dynamics going on. Reflect on what it all means for what you've got planned next and how you might need to adjust. Give yourself permission to step out of an evaluative role as students talk. An evaluative stance is not a fruitful place for the kind of listening, observing, and reflecting that makes us the best teachers we can be for the students who people our classrooms.

## The Goal Is Independence

Giving students space to talk takes time, and it is most definitely *not* efficient. It's messy. Students may spend valuable class time talking about something that's not that helpful to the writer sharing their work. Or they may give feedback that we ourselves might not deem important. Students will eventually get to the heart of the work, and it will be far more effective for *their* learning if we support them while they talk together to make their *own* way there. If you're looking for instructional methods that try to rein in the messiness of student-led learning, you're reading the wrong book!

It was October of 2016. Many of my seniors would be voting in their first presidential election in just a few weeks. I had planned the same conversation I usually did at this point in the semester, hoping it would inspire more open-mindedness about the different complexities of the social issues they had each chosen to explore for a research-based writing task.

But that particular fall, ramping up to that particular presidential election, developing skills to navigate conversations about contentious topics had taken on new urgency. Our text to consider was a TED Talk by Kathryn Schulz, "On Being Wrong." We watched it. They read the transcript. They reflected in their notebooks as a *start small* preparation task for our whole-class discussion: what do you think are the top three most important concepts of Schulz's explanation?

As I circulated around the room casually scanning for completed prep tasks, I asked them to *seek connections* by talking about their notes with the people around them. I could hear what students had identified as important concepts floating around the room.

Prep task checked, it was time to start our conversation to build collective understanding about the TED Talk. Once the students got settled either at the conference table in the center or on the outside ready to listen, I threw out an invitation to start talking: “What ideas from Schulz’s TED Talk will you take forward with you—as you become an adult who votes?”

There were a few beats of weighty silence as the students looked at each other and at me as they realized that I wasn’t just inviting conversation about Schulz’s text. I was inviting them to *take action* with conversation about our increasingly chaotic political context and how they might navigate the ever-growing chasm between people who disagree.

I receded into the outside circle to listen and let those who had chosen to speak take the conversation where they wished.

On that particular day, they taught me a few things.

They showed me how to disagree respectfully, how to listen to each other, how to show others they’ve been heard. They showed me how to put Schulz’s explanation into practice as a map to navigate the moments of tension that emerge when we run up against someone who disagrees. They showed me how to take a step back and interrogate one’s own stance.

They showed me how to connect with kindness and respect across differences.

And they left me hopeful.

When we show students how to drive classroom talk and invite them to talk about topics that matter to them, we provide opportunities for them to grow critical discussion skills for life.

CHAPTER 5

# INVITE STUDENTS TO DRIVE ASSESSMENT AND GRADING

> *Ranking. Norming. Objectivity. Uniformity. Standardization. Measurement. Outcomes. Quality. Data. Performance. Metrics. Scores. Excellence. Mastery. Rigor. There is no room for student agency to breathe in a system of incessant grading, ranking, and sorting.*
>
> —Stommel, 2020, 27

Our classrooms must be safe spaces for students to take the risks involved in genuinely reading, in writing about what really matters to them, in stumbling through their ideas as they are forming, and in talking with others earnestly. Cornelius Minor reminds us, "Creating a space where kids feel safe means we must create a space where we share power" (Minor, 2019). Traditional grading practices center power on teachers; we can reframe grading as a critical place to turn over power to students. Otherwise, we undermine all of the other student-driven practices in this book.

The shift toward humanizing classroom assessment practices is a journey, one I will always be on. Since writing *Point-Less: An English Teacher's Guide to More Meaningful Grading* (2020), I realized I could see what the work looked like more clearly than my students could. I had a good idea about how learning generally progresses for each learning goal—which knowledge and skills were foundational and how learning grew from there. I knew exactly which learning behaviors enable success for each learning goal. But my students didn't necessarily have all of this knowledge, leaving them without concrete ideas about how to hone their learning behaviors and making their personal progress monitoring more difficult. This left my students dependent on me to guide their learning rather than driving it themselves.

Zaretta Hammond explains, "Dependent learners have been conditioned to be passive when it comes to making decisions about their learning moves. They have relied on the teacher to tell them what to do next. If they are to become more independent, we have to provide them with the tools" (2015, 100). Over the past few years, I've developed some new tools to help my students drive their own assessment more: learning progressions that spell out the kinds of things students can focus on to grow toward each objective and descriptive rubrics that indicate what it takes to complete the work of a task fully. Both tools help students better visualize the *work* of learning.

I've also come to understand the pieces of the approach that seem to be most critical to students truly driving assessment and grading [Figure 5.1]. First, we can turn over some key tasks to students to drive on their own: goal setting, ongoing reflection, and evaluation. Next, we can focus on holding students accountable for doing the work while making sure they can see clearly how they are learning and growing. Finally, we can provide clear guidelines for students to select their own final grades.

## The Point-Less Approach

If you've come to this book after reading *Point-Less*, you'll recognize what underpins the grading strategies in this chapter. If you haven't read *Point-Less*, it sketches out a path to the final semester grade where students set their own learning goals, monitor their progress, and write the story of their learning journey at semester's end when they select their final grades. The gradebook tracks whether or not students are doing the work and collects assessment data that students can examine to track their own progress. The focus is on process over product, growth toward individual goals over mastery of the exact same standards, and the actual *work* of learning rather than the points-for-compliance exchange that classrooms orbit on in traditional grading.

Whether you're familiar with the Point-Less approach or not, use the QR code here to link to a hyperdoc resource that shows, week-by-week, the steps of navigating a Point-Less semester and includes links to the necessary resources along the way, including the new tools I share in this chapter.

| Things to teach students to do for themselves: | Things teachers can do so it's possible for students to drive: |
|---|---|
| • Setting their own goals for learning.<br>• Strategies for ongoing reflection.<br>• Evaluating their own work. | • Hold students accountable for *doing* the work.<br>• Help students see their own progress toward their learning goals.<br>• Provide clear guidelines for final grade selection. |

**Figure 5.1** Stepping Aside So Students Can Drive Grading and Assessment

## Teach Students How to Set Their Own Goals for Learning

Our students have goals. But, in order to take the wheel in ways that set them up for success, they'll need a set of learning goals that clarify the content of the course, learning progressions that help them to imagine how a journey might progress toward each learning goal, and behaviors they can practice that will enable them to truly drive.

### *A Clear Set of Learning Goals*

There should be no mystery in our students' minds about the learning that our courses target. But the documents that spell out standards and curricular expectations are overwhelming. The Common Core State Standards list over sixty individual standards for each grade level in secondary language arts. And then there are specific curriculum documents for a particular school district or the Advanced Placement (AP) or International Baccalaureate (IB) curriculum documents to navigate, too. It's our job to sort through those documents and make sure we are teaching what we need to.

But a clear list of learning goals—no more than ten—is more manageable for students (and for us!). Something we can all look at together to guide our work, that makes sense to students, that makes the work of the class look manageable. Here's the list of learning goals for the tenth-grade class I teach:

| | | |
|---|---|---|
| **Content goals** | 1. | Consider an author's choices as you read to figure out what you think a text means overall. |
| | 2. | Examine individual words closely to derive meaning in a text. |
| | 3. | Write narratives, arguments, and informative pieces to effectively say what you think about topics that matter to you. |
| | 4. | Revise extensively to improve a piece of writing using mentor texts and reader feedback. |
| | 5. | Engage in meaningful conversation with others (speaking and listening) to figure out what you think. |
| | 6. | Successfully speak aloud your ideas in class. |
| | 7. | Gather and use information from a variety of sources to develop and support your ideas. |
| **Successful human being goals (learning behaviors)** | 8. | Demonstrate successful student habits. |
| | 9. | Practice effective self-reflection, self-evaluation, and metacognition. |
| | 10. | Be a positive community member. |

Goals 1–7 are content goals; they capture the curricular expectations in my state and school district for tenth-grade language arts. Goals 8, 9, and 10 I call "successful human being goals." They reflect learning behaviors more than the skills and knowledge embedded in the content goals. To get to a similar list, start with your values about teaching reading and writing, and use those as a lens to sort through your many curriculum expectations. We do this every day anyway. There's never enough time to accomplish everything expected of us; we make choices about what to focus on in the time we have. (See Chapter 2 of *Point-Less* for steps to follow to articulate and use your values to narrow your curriculum expectations.)

For any concern that this short list might not reflect the full range of the curriculum expectations, I keep an expanded document that shows exactly which standards and curricular expectations connect to each learning goal. It's all there. But this short list is more manageable to position at the center of the classroom, and it enables collective power through a shared vision about the purpose of the class.

### *Clearly Articulate Learning Progressions for Each of the Learning Goals*

Students need to have a sense of what the work and learning actually look like for each of the course's learning goals. I've started using learning

progressions for this. According to the UNESCO International Bureau of Education, learning progressions describe the "increasing levels of difficulty and complexity" that come along with learning particular knowledge and skills. Learning progressions emphasize that learning is not about covering content. They remind teachers that we need to think of the "continuum of how learning develops," and they make for more meaningfully aligned instruction and assessment (*Learning Progression*, n.d.). They also help students take the wheel by showing what they might focus on, step by step, to grow their skills and knowledge.

Here's an example learning progression for the second tenth-grade learning goal mentioned earlier:

| **Content Goal #2:**<br>➔ **Examine individual words closely to derive meaning in a text.** | | **Tools we'll use to practice these skills** |
|---|---|---|
| **Foundational**<br>⇩<br>⇩<br>**Growing your skills**<br>⇩<br>⇩<br>**Extending your skills** | 1. Pause and note individual words.<br>2. Capture your original thinking.<br>3. Keep track of where in the text the words come from.<br>4. Identify figurative language.<br>5. Use context to puzzle out the meaning and/or impact of a word or phrase.<br>6. Analyze the impact of figurative language on meaning. | • OTAs<br>• Rambling thoughts |

The progression starts with what's foundational—the critical actions that all other actions build from. The two most foundational actions toward examining individual words closely to derive meaning in a text are to first pause when there's a word or two to ponder and write them down. Second is to capture some original thinking about the word/s. If students are not doing those two essential actions, nothing else in the learning progression is possible.

It's important to also indicate the tools students will use in class to practice each learning goal. The primary strategies where students will practice looking closely at individual words are original thought annotations (OTAs) and rambling thoughts (see Chapter 2).

A learning progression offers an opportunity to expand a learning goal with a bit more detail than appears in the short list of course learning goals, which you can see with the last three items in the example learning progression. They reflect the prioritized standards for tenth grade in my district, where there's an emphasis on identifying and making sense of figurative language.

Learning progressions like this are useful for students in several ways:

- Self-evaluating one's location in the learning progression for the content goals can help students make informed decisions about which goals they want to target themselves in goal setting.
- As students are setting their own goals, they can use learning progressions to help them describe both a baseline for where they are starting and a vision for what their success could look like.
- As students self-monitor their progress throughout the term, they can refer back to the learning progressions to see how they are moving toward each of the goals they set.

And learning progressions are useful for us because:

- They become a road map we can look at when we talk with students about their learning progress in conferences.
- They remind us to plan for opportunities that give students ample time to practice the work outlined by each learning progression and to plan for assessments students can use to determine their movement along the learning progressions.

Writing learning progressions takes time and effort. It's difficult to explicitly articulate knowledge we carry implicitly in our minds. My observations of past students working with the course's learning goals helped me think about what was foundational and what grew from there. I also turned to the structure of our curriculum for some help, like for goal #3, which you can see if you look ahead at Figure 5.4. I positioned some items about writing narrative at the end of the learning progression. Because the narrative writing invitations come in the last two units of our school year, it made sense to place them toward the end of that particular learning progression.

Learning progressions offer a framework and vision of what's possible, a shared understanding to sit at the center of the classroom. The point is to share knowledge with students about what the learning really looks like so they can better drive their own journeys through it. Don't present the learning progressions to students as some kind of lock-step way to move through the content for each learning goal. Allow for some flexibility and nuance as students navigate authentically through the progression.

### *Clearly Articulate the Learning Behaviors that Support the Learning Goals*

No matter how much I try to cajole my students to read the instructions I craft with such care, still they often charge forward in their work without checking the instructions in detail. Sending back incomplete work to finish is annoying for students and for me. But students might not realize this behavior actually gets in the way of their success. We can describe specific behaviors that support learning, actions students can choose to be successful.

Particular behaviors directly connect to students driving their learning. We can spell out those behaviors for them. Notice how the columns on the learning behavior document shown in Figure 5.2 encompass four "levels" for student behaviors: not doing the work, getting in your own way, doing the work, and driving the work. Following instructions carefully falls under goal #8, "demonstrate successful student habits." "Assuming you know the instructions without reading through them first" falls under "getting in your own way" because it's a behavior students often don't even realize is keeping them from reaching their goal.

This document is not a set-in-stone grade declaration. It's a framework to help students to think about when they are choosing learning behaviors that will get in the way of their own success and when they are choosing learning behaviors that will lead to learning.

For both the learning progressions and the learning behaviors, every item represents something students can choose to do (or not), showing them that success is within their control. It's not about inherent talent or intelligence. If they choose to do the work—the actions outlined in the learning progressions and the behaviors outlined in the learning behaviors—they will learn.

## Learning *Behaviors* for CP10 Learning Goals

| Grade range⇨ | F-ish | D-ish | C-ish | B-ish | A-ish |
|---|---|---|---|---|---|

| Learning Goal⇩ | Not doing the work | Getting in your own way | First, ***doing*** the work... | ...to be ***driving*** the work |
|---|---|---|---|---|
| **EI GHT:**<br>Demonstrate successful student habits. | ☐ Not showing up to class.<br>☐ Not doing the work.<br>☐ Fake reading and/or only using online summaries.<br>☐ Not looking at instructions.<br>☐ Never asking for help.<br>☐ Letting your phone control how you spend your time.<br>☐ Never having your laptop and/or writer's notebook .<br>☐ Not checking LMS/gradebook.<br>☐ Letting AI chatbots/other sources write for you. (cheating!)<br>THE ONLY WAY TO FAI L<br>☐ One or more major task is "missing" in the gradebook. | ☐ Being late to class.<br>☐ Turning in work late.<br>☐ Sometimes not doing the work.<br>☐ Assuming you know the instructions.<br>☐ Rarely checking LMS/gradebook.<br>☐ Forgetting to put your phone in your assigned pocket.<br>☐ Doing other stuff on your laptop.<br>☐ Forgetting your laptop and/or writer's notebook.<br>☐ Doing minimal conferences.<br>☐ Writing whatever to get it done.<br>☐ Not prioritizing time for reading and/or writing.<br>☐ Not trusting that your own ideas are strong enough. | ☐ Asking questions/for help.<br>☐ Doing work thoughtfully and on time.<br>☐ Following instructions carefully.<br>☐ Using rambling thoughts to explore what you're thinking.<br>☐ Having your writer's notebook and/or laptop every day.<br>☐ Looking at LMS/gradebook to keep track of your work.<br>☐ Putting your phone in your assigned pocket every day.<br>☐ Coming to conferences ready to talk about your work.<br>☐ Choosing writing topics that matter to you.<br>☐ Making time to read and write. | ☐ Doing work on your own without the teacher's prompting.<br>☐ Writing rambling thoughts until you've figured out something that matters to you.<br>☐ Keeping your completed work percentage is in the high 90s.<br>☐ Actively managing your phone so it doesn't control you, in and out of class.<br>☐ Seeking out more conferences than required to discuss what YOU want to talk about.<br>☐ Having your laptop in class, charged, every day.<br>☐ Writing to explore what you think about the topics you find on your own |
| **NI NE:**<br>Practice effective self-reflection, self-evaluation, and metacognition. | ☐ Not setting or tracking your learning goals.<br>☐ Not writing writer's memos. | ☐ Setting learning goals that don't really matter to you.<br>☐ Putting whatever on weekly learning progress OTAs.<br>☐ Writing writer's memos just to get them done.<br>☐ Not using a rubric or checklist to guide revision. | ☐ Setting learning goals that matter to you.<br>☐ Writing thoughtful weekly learning progress OTAs.<br>☐ Looking at LMS/gradebook for evidence of your progress.<br>☐ Writing careful writer's memos.<br>☐ Using a rubric/checklist to guide revision. | ☐ Doing additional learning progress OTAs on your own.<br>☐ Actively monitoring classroom assessment data sources to track your learning progress.<br>☐ Reflecting about your writing/revision in writer's memos.<br>☐ Using a rubric or checklist on your own to guide revision. |
| **TEN:**<br>Be a positive community member. | ☐ Being a negative impact on the classroom community.<br>☐ Not paying any attention to what's going on in class.<br>☐ Not talking to your group. | ☐ Distracting others.<br>☐ Letting your group be unfocused.<br>☐ Paying little attention to class.<br>☐ Giving minimal feedback to others on their writing.<br>☐ Using shared digital spaces to be "funny," not focused.<br>☐ Assuming that no one wants to hear what you have to say. | ☐ Paying attention so you know what you should be doing.<br>☐ Being focused in your group.<br>☐ Offering helpful feedback to others on their writing.<br>☐ Remaining on task in shared digital spaces. | ☐ Always knowing what you should be doing during class.<br>☐ Keeping your group focused.<br>☐ Cultivating a culture of feedback in your group so that you turn to each other for feedback on your own.<br>☐ Using shared digital spaces to lift up the learning of everyone. |

Figure 5.2 Learning Behaviors for Tenth-Grade Successful Human Being Goals. This document shows students the actual learning behaviors to practice in order to learn the content outlined by the learning progressions. I add the grade band across the top to suggest to students that—generally—there are particular learning behaviors to engage to help them get to whatever grade they are planning to select at semester's end. I ask students to check off the items that describe their current behaviors, so they can see for themselves where they have room to grow.

### *Invite Students to Make a Plan for Their Own Learning Journeys*

Once we have crafted a tight list of learning goals, clarified the work of the goals with learning progressions, and articulated for students the behaviors that will support their success, we are ready for students to use these tools to make a plan for the learning they want to do, the foundation for student-driven grading. Before we dive into that part of the process, let's take a quick look at Kai's plan for taking on three of the tenth-grade learning goals [Figure 5.3].

| Goal in your own words | Where you're starting | What you want to work on along the way | Where you want to end up |
|---|---|---|---|
| Goal 1 (content goal #1):<br>Consider how specific details/ moments/ passages achieve a text's purpose. | I'm able to read and determine the theme as well as analyze and evaluate the book. | • Look back at parts of the book, the details and moments can make a difference in the purpose.<br>• Further analyze important parts to lead to the overall purpose. | I'd like to end up seeing the purpose of a text without trying too hard and using what I can to do that. |
| Goal 2 (content goal #5): Summarize agreement and disagreement in group discussion. | In group discussions, I've been able to share out, make connections with others, and expand the discussion with questions. | • At the end of discussion, debrief what the final thoughts are.<br>• Ask people what the final opinions are when we're done discussing. | Knowing what everyone's agreements and disagreements are by the time we're done. So that I can realize the effects of my ideas. |
| Goal 3 (his own goal built off of content goal #6):<br>To trust that my writing ideas are strong and good enough to write about. | I'm able to write about my own ideas but I end up overthinking that it may not be good enough. | • Start elaborating certain details to make parts more interesting and intriguing.<br>• Trusting that my stories and topics are good enough. People won't judge them. | I want to end up having trust in my topics and not letting the overthinking end up affecting what it ends up looking like. |

**Figure 5.3** Kai's Plan for Learning and Growth

Kai is a pretty thoughtful tenth grader, but Kai's work here is not terribly unusual for my students, no matter the grade or course. Given the right support, all students can set their own goals and chart their own path for pursuing them. To see how the learning progressions helped Kai in his goal setting, Figure 5.4 shows the self-evaluation he did before determining which learning goals he wanted to work on. I asked students to check off the boxes that described things they could do with confidence.

In Kai's plan for learning and growth [Figure 5.3], he articulated his first personal goal using the language at the end of the learning progression for goal #1. For his second personal goal, he pulled language directly from the boxes he did not check in the learning progression for goal #5. It seems that goal #7 is the one Kai needs to work on the most according to how many boxes he did not check off in its learning progression. But his confidence in what he writes about took precedence in his thinking. Note that the only box Kai did not check off in the learning progression for goal #6 was the first one, trusting that his ideas are worth talking about. Perhaps his inability to check that box with confidence made him think about how he feels about his ideas when writing, thus leading to his third personal learning goal. The fact that Kai repurposed some language in goal #6 to craft his own writing goal shows agency here. He has evaluated his needs as a writer, identified something he wants to work on, and designed his own learning goal to target that work.

Students will not be as successful in choosing and personalizing learning goals until they know what the work of the class looks like. I don't show them the learning goals right at the start of the semester. Delaying their goal setting a few weeks into the school year gives students time to become familiar with the work of the class before they decide what they want to work on. It also provides important time for you to study your class to determine parameters around goal setting that will best support a particular group of students. For example, you might choose one content goal that everyone needs to work on so that you can work through the goal setting and planning together, focusing on that one goal as a shared example. You could also provide a bit of a framework—perhaps ask students to choose one reading goal, one writing goal, and one successful human being goal (or something similar).

# Learning *Progressions* for CP10 Learning Goals

| Learning Goal ⇨ | ONE: Consider an author's choices as you read to figure out what YOU think a text means overall.<br>**OTAs, rambling thoughts** | TWO: Examine individual words closely to derive meaning in a text.<br>**OTAs, rambling thoughts** | THREE: Write narratives, arguments, and informative pieces, effectively saying what you think about topics that matter to you.<br>**weekly writing** | FOUR: Revise extensively to improve a piece of writing.<br>**weekly writing, revision tasks, writer's memos** | FIVE: Engage in meaningful conversation with others to figure out what YOU think.<br>**small group/whole class conversations** | SIX: Successfully speak aloud your ideas to class.<br>**daily share outs, whole-class conversation, informal presentations** | SEVEN: Gather and use information from a variety of sources to develop and support your ideas.<br>**weekly writing, citation tool** |
|---|---|---|---|---|---|---|---|
| **Foundational skills**<br>⇩<br>⇩<br>⇩<br>⇩<br>**Growing your skills**<br>⇩<br>⇩<br>⇩<br>⇩<br>**Extending your skills** | ☑ Read carefully.<br>☑ Re-read when necessary.<br>☐ Summarize a text objectively.<br>☑ Determine the theme/central idea/purpose.<br>☐ Consider how the text's structure impacts meaning.<br>☑ In literature, analyze development of<br>☑ characters.<br>☑ plot.<br>☑ theme.<br>☑ In non-fiction texts, evaluate<br>☑ claims.<br>☑ evidence.<br>☑ reasoning.<br>☐ Consider how specific details/moments/passages achieve a text's purpose. | ☑ Pause and note individual words.<br>☑ Capture your original thinking.<br>☑ Keep track of where in the text the words come from.<br>☑ Identify figurative language.<br>☑ Use context to puzzle out the meaning and/or impact of a word or phrase.<br>☑ Analyze the impact of figurative language on meaning. | ☑ Develop informative writing with specific details.<br>☐ Conclude effectively in a final section.<br>☑ Develop argumentative writing with specific claims, evidence, and explanation.<br>☑ Find your own topics that meet the goals of the task.<br>☑ Build an argumentative thesis based on evidence first.<br>☐ Use plot events to develop a narrative.<br>☑ Build a story from a character who wants something, navigating obstacles in the way (conflict). | ☑ Don't just fix errors: replace, add, delete, and re-order as you revise.<br>☑ Articulate the changes you want to make in revision.<br>☑ Describe the changes you actually make in revision.<br>☐ Use one of the mentor texts provided in class.<br>☑ Choose a convenient reader for feedback.<br>☑ Drive an AI chatbot as a helpful personal editor.<br>☐ Find your own mentor text.<br>☑ Choose the exact right reader(s) for feedback.<br>☑ Revise extensively. | ☑ Use each other's names.<br>☑ Listen to the ideas of others.<br>☑ Invite others to share their thinking.<br>☑ Ask others to clarify.<br>☑ Respond to questions thoughtfully.<br>☑ Pose questions to expand the discussion.<br>☐ Make connections between ideas.<br>☐ Summarize agreement and disagreement.<br>☑ Support ideas with examples/evidence.<br>☑ Make space for differing ideas.<br>☑ Build understanding together. | ☐ Trust that your ideas are worth listening to.<br>☑ Share your thinking in conversation with your group.<br>☑ Make space for others to speak.<br>☑ Choose to speak when invited to share your thinking aloud with the whole class.<br>☑ Choose to speak in seminar conversations.<br>☑ Volunteer to share out to the whole class about your group's conversation.<br>☑ Seek out more opportunities to share your thinking aloud. | ☑ Seek research sources when included in a specific task's instructions.<br>☑ Evaluate source credibility.<br>☐ Integrate research into your writing effectively (avoiding plagiarism).<br>☐ Document research following a standard format.<br>☐ Seek and use research sources even when not included in a specific task's instructions.<br>☐ Develop your own system and strategies for keeping track of research. |

**Bolded and highlighted** = specific tools we're using to practice these skills.

Figure 5.4 Kai's Self-Evaluation on the Learning Progressions
Kai checked off the boxes for the items he felt he could do with confidence.

IF YOU FIND YOURSELF THINKING...

If students each only focus on a handful of the learning goals for grading, their final grades will not reflect how they're doing on all of the required curriculum.

CONSIDER: The traditional grading system expects us to produce one letter grade that captures:

MASTERY TOWARDS ALL THE STANDARDS
STUDENT GROWTH
ATHLETIC ELIGIBILITY
PREPAREDNESS FOR THE NEXT CLASS
A+
COLLEGE READINESS
CAREER READINESS
even...
CAR INSURANCE DISCOUNTS

But it's impossible for one letter grade to capture all of that.

Instead, the path to the final grade should be MEANINGFUL for our students first and foremost.

Even though students might plan to focus on only three goals in their plan for learning and growth...

...you're still teaching all ten. All students are working on all ten.

Putting students in the driver's seat of grading means shifting what the overall grade means to them.

Rather than waiting for the teacher to determine a grade that evaluates their achievement toward a set of external standards...

I'm giving you a B-

I'm selecting an A...

...students can select a grade that reflects the learning journey they planned on their own.

Student goal setting gets students invested in their own learning and growth.

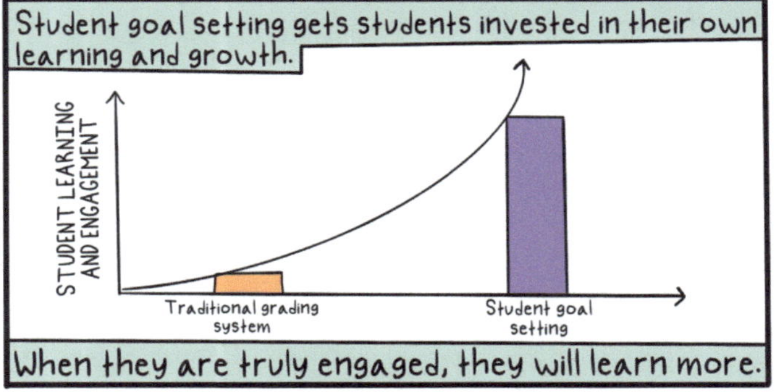


When they are truly engaged, they will learn more.

**Figure 5.5** Backseat Driver Warning

## Teach Students Strategies for Ongoing Reflection

Setting goals is only part of the equation. We must invite students to revisit their goals frequently and teach them how to reflect. This is the second key task for them to drive their own grading and assessment. I find that a learning goal check once per week or so is about the right frequency. There are umpteen ways we can teach students to reflect on their learning and growth. No matter how you invite students to reflect, ask them to collect small moments that help them to see their progress on their goals.

Students can use the same simple sticky note protocol of OTAs (see Chapter 2) to track what they notice about their own learning. Model for students how to use OTAs effectively to monitor their progress. On the same day each week, share your own learning goal OTAs. Point out the kinds of small things you're noticing and talk through what you're thinking about those small things. Figure 5.6 shows my collection of learning goal OTAs that I shared with my sophomores for January–March of 2023. I always write my own plan for learning and growth with goals that are authentic to the reading and writing work I'm attempting in my life beyond school. I make sure my goals connect at least loosely with the list of learning goals for the class, showing students that the course goals capture reading and writing work humans actually do.

After sharing my most recent learning goal OTA(s) with the class, I invite a few quiet minutes for students to revisit their plans for learning and growth and do one or two learning goal OTAs. At "I noticed," they write something specific connected to one of their goals—a data point, a moment of success, a moment that wasn't successful. At "I think," they write to explore what that reveals toward their personal learning goal. If there's time, inviting a few students to share a learning goal OTA provides some relatable whole-class instruction. It also doesn't take long to make my way around the classroom to look at one learning goal OTA from each student, weaving in quick, one-on-one instructional moments as needed.

For student reflection, you can also harness a learning management system (like Google Classroom, Schoology, or the like). Create an assignment for students to turn in their plans for learning and growth (on an electronic document or a photo of the paper version in their notebooks) and then each week or so, ask students to go back to that assignment,

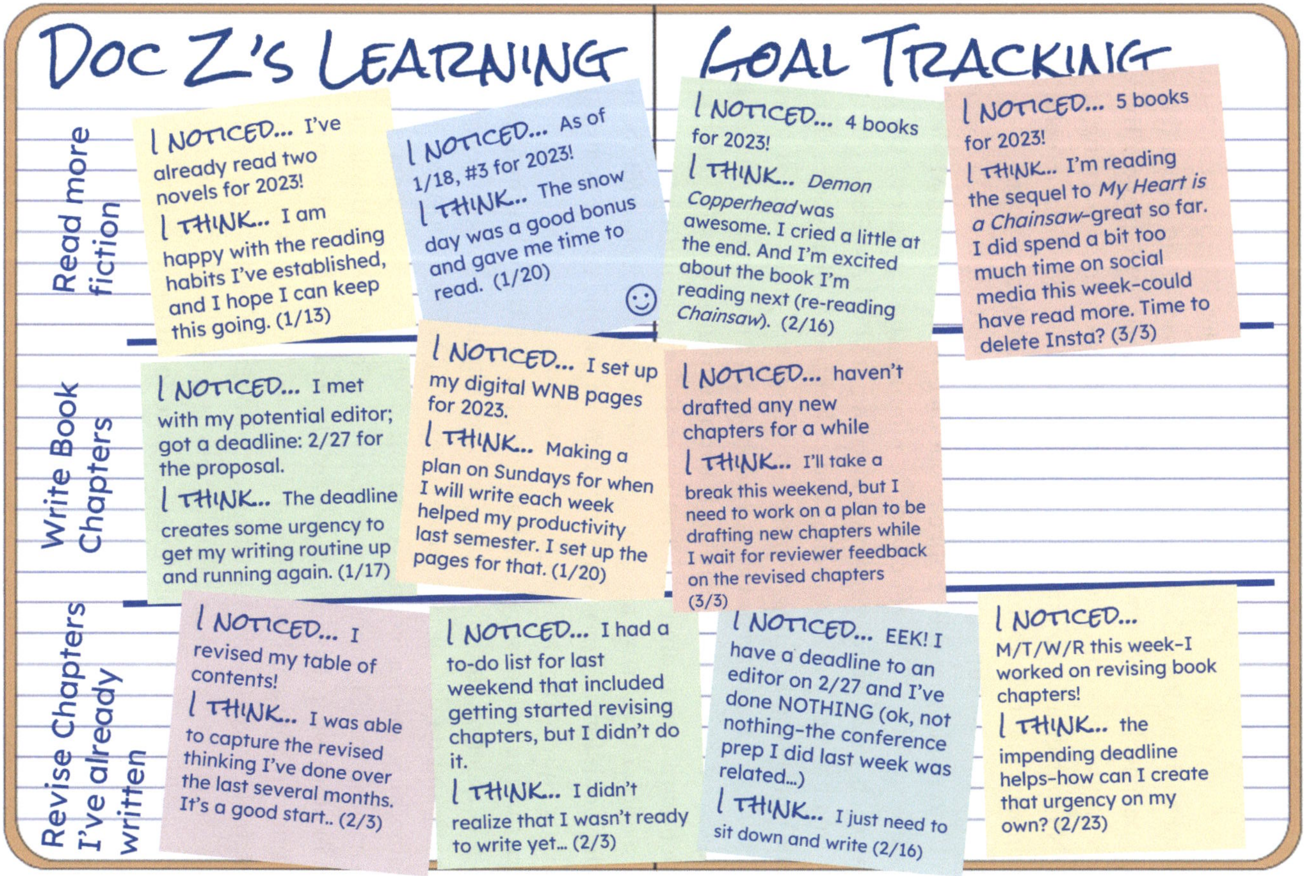

Doc Z's Learning Goal Tracking
Read more fiction
I NOTICED... I've already read two novels for 2023!
I THINK... I am happy with the reading habits I've established, and I hope I can keep this going. (1/13)
I NOTICED... As of 1/18, #3 for 2023!
I THINK... The snow day was a good bonus and gave me time to read. (1/20)
I NOTICED... 4 books for 2023!
I THINK... Demon Copperhead was awesome. I cried a little at the end. And I'm excited about the book I'm reading next (re-reading Chainsaw). (2/16)
I NOTICED... 5 books for 2023!
I THINK... I'm reading the sequel to My Heart is a Chainsaw–great so far. I did spend a bit too much time on social media this week–could have read more. Time to delete Insta? (3/3)
Write Book Chapters
I NOTICED... I met with my potential editor; got a deadline: 2/27 for the proposal.
I THINK... The deadline creates some urgency to get my writing routine up and running again. (1/17)
I NOTICED... I set up my digital WNB pages for 2023.
I THINK... Making a plan on Sundays for when I will write each week helped my productivity last semester. I set up the pages for that. (1/20)
I NOTICED... haven't drafted any new chapters for a while
I THINK... I'll take a break this weekend, but I need to work on a plan to be drafting new chapters while I wait for reviewer feedback on the revised chapters (3/3)
Revise Chapters I've already written
I NOTICED... I revised my table of contents!
I THINK... I was able to capture the revised thinking I've done over the last several months. It's a good start.. (2/3)
I NOTICED... I had a to-do list for last weekend that included getting started revising chapters, but I didn't do it.
I THINK... I didn't realize that I wasn't ready to write yet... (2/3)
I NOTICED... EEK! I have a deadline to an editor on 2/27 and I've done NOTHING (ok, not nothing–the conference prep I did last week was related...)
I THINK... I just need to sit down and write (2/16)
I NOTICED... M/T/W/R this week–I worked on revising book chapters!
I THINK... the impending deadline helps–how can I create that urgency on my own? (2/23)

**Figure 5.6** Doc Z's Learning Goal OTAs
I created this on a slide deck mirroring how students could use their notebooks to collect learning goal OTAs.

look at their plans attached there, and write a comment about one recent moment that connects to any of their three goals. Ask them to describe the moment and then reflect on what it reveals about their progress. Look at their comments and write a quick note back, "Thank you for your week 23 learning goal reflection! Awesome that you wrote about a topic that matters to you." Just like with the learning goal OTAs collected in a notebook, by semester's end, the long string of comments is a rich collection of their reflection. But an advantage to this strategy is that you can see their reflections without having to collect their notebooks, providing an ever-expanding assessment resource to inform instruction.

You wouldn't need to use a learning management system for this. A shared document would suffice, one that students revisit every week and add on another note of reflection. But I've found that having their reflective notes right there as comments in the learning management system means I don't have to open up a document for each student each week—it saves me time.

## Teach Students How to Evaluate Their Own Work

Evaluation means examining students' work up against some set of standards. It underpins traditional grading, where teachers constantly tell students—via points or grades or rubric scores—how well they are doing. Constant evaluation by the teacher does not serve learners well: "it turns out that hearing how well we've done (typically from someone in a position of power) often doesn't lead us to improve" (Kohn et al., 2022). Whenever there's a need to determine how well students have done something, we can turn over that evaluation to students.

For example, if you teach an AP or IB course, there are rubrics available for how students' work will be evaluated on the external AP and IB exams. Students should know any rubrics that will evaluate their work in a high-stakes situation. When I began teaching AP Literature years ago, I used AP's 9-point rubric to evaluate students' essays in my class and converted students' rubric scores to a grade for the gradebook. This made every essay a high-stakes event, which created stress and anxiety on a literary analysis task students had little practice with before my class. Having a grade at stake also tamped down their creativity, making it difficult for them to take the kinds of risks that lead to learning.

If the rubric score is not a grade in the traditional sense, then other possibilities open up, like peer evaluation. The more students talk with each other as they use the rubric to evaluate each other's work, the better they will grow to know the rubric and the work it outlines. Student self-evaluation also becomes possible. Their self-determined rubric scores compared to our own rubric scores can reveal places to lean in with instruction.

Imagine you discover that students are rating their use of topic sentences to structure an argument much higher than you determine via your own rubric scoring. That points to misunderstanding—of the rubric and possibly of the role of topic sentences. Now you know what you need to teach next to help them improve. With frequent modeling and conversation around using the rubric to self- and peer-evaluate students' work, they will learn the rubric (and the work it outlines) well. We can position any evaluative rubric we need or want to use in this way, making it a powerful tool for students to monitor their own progress.

## Hold Students Accountable for the Doing of the Work

"Do the things to learn the stuff" has become my weekly reminder to students that success is simple. If they aren't doing the work—fully and thoughtfully—it will be difficult for them to learn and grow.

"Do the things to learn the stuff" is also clear shorthand to remind us what to anchor student-driven grading on. We can turn over "learning the stuff" to students—which is what this chapter has been about so far: teaching them how to set their own goals for learning, reflect consistently on their growth, and evaluate their own work. Helping students see clearly if they are "doing the things," then, can become *our* focus.

If we must quantify something in a required gradebook (and I'm in a school where I must), then we can recast the overall gradebook percentage as a completed work percentage, a reflection of how completely and fully students are actually doing the work. We can also use clear rubrics that describe the work (rather than evaluating it) so students know the exact actions they need to do to complete the work.

### *Help Students See How Fully and Completely They Are Doing the Work*

If the numbers you're likely required to have in your gradebook are evaluative—meaning that they evaluate your students' work against some standard of quality—then the overall gradebook percentage is an ever-present reminder to students about how "good" they are. Constant evaluation gets in the way of a healthy teacher/learner relationship and locates power with the teacher. A gradebook that quantifies nothing more than how much of the work students are doing sends a different message, one that learners have control over. It is within their power to do the work or not (with flexibility and exceptions for extenuating circumstances, of course).

Even though the overall gradebook percentage is not a "grade" in my class, I still work within a wider system that operates on traditional grading. It's important that when an administrator, parent, or colleague who supports students in my class looks at my gradebook, they see something familiar. Having to constantly explain to those stakeholders how to make sense of a gradebook that appears to be out of the norm throws up potential resistance. Rather than setting myself up to constantly explain to other stakeholders how to make sense of unfamiliar gradebook data, I make sure it *looks* familiar and then remind my students every week that it *means* something different. It simply reflects whether or not students are keeping up with the work. It's only one data point the students will consider when selecting their grade at semester's end.

### *What to Put in the Score Boxes in the Gradebook*

Quantifying how much of the work students are doing also simplifies gradebook data entry. All you need is a metric to represent complete, partial, and missing. It could be 10/10 for complete, 7/10 for partial, 0/10 for missing. As long as students know what the numbers mean, that's what matters most.

Knowing that my school community thinks about the overall gradebook percentage as a grade in a traditional sense, I use it deliberately to communicate with students and other stakeholders if a student has fallen behind on some critical work. The most important assignments for my class go into a gradebook category called "can't be missing to get credit for the class," and that category makes up 60 percent to 80 percent of the overall percentage (depending on the class). A missing assignment in that category will impact the overall percentage significantly, hopefully creating some urgency around the student to get that important work turned in.

If students know that the overall gradebook percentage reflects how fully they are completing the work, they can use it as a quick check to make sure everything's in and complete. Anything less than 100 percent (or close to it) signals that they've got something missing or partially complete they need to take care of.

### *Use Descriptive Rubrics to Show Students Clearly What Complete Work Means*

For much of the routine, ongoing work we ask of students, we can check it off as done or not done, even by just glancing at it. In fact, most of this type of work I don't even collect. I just have students show it to me in class and I check it off on a roster on a clipboard (which also gives me additional opportunities to have brief conversations with students). And if I'm not collecting the work, I don't need to go through it later, which saves me time.

Other tasks demand more than a quick glance. For those, we can provide clear rubrics that describe what will determine if the task is complete or not. Take rambling thoughts (see Chapter 2) for example. My rambling thoughts instructions include six steps, each step intended to engage students in the *process* of writing to form connections across a few small ideas to build bigger ones. I've turned those six process steps into a simple rubric [Figure 5.7] that describes the task. Such a rubric makes it quick and easy to determine if a task is complete or partially complete. This rubric is also something *students* can use themselves to determine whether or not they have completed the task fully.

| **Status of work** | |
|---|---|
| **Complete**<br>All categories below are checked off "Yes!" | **Partial**<br>Keep working and resubmit ASAP. |
| **Two-page notebook spread** | |
| Yes!<br>Not yet | Start with a blank two-page spread in your notebook. |
| **Ideas to work with** | |
| Yes!<br>Not yet | Select 3 to 4 OTAs to ramble about and put them on the left-side page. |
| **Text and date** | |
| Yes!<br>Not yet | Write the title of the text you're rambling about and today's date at the top of the left-side page. |
| **Prewriting** | |
| Yes!<br>Not yet | Jot some notes in between and around the OTAs on the left-side page to start to explore how they are connected. |
| **Ramble** | |
| Yes!<br>Not yet | On the right-side page, write to explore the connections between your OTAs and to build your thinking. Keep writing until you figure something out. |
| **Title** | |
| Yes!<br>Not yet | Read over your rambling and write (on the top of the right-side page) a short title that captures what you ended up writing about. |

**Figure 5.7** Descriptive Rubric for Rambling Thoughts

Descriptive rubrics are essentially the assignment instructions in rubric form. Many educators (and assessment experts!) argue that rubrics should never be just the assignment instructions, that they should focus on the skills and content a particular task targets. But it depends on the purpose of the rubric. A classroom moving away from traditional grading places a stronger emphasis on students doing the actual *work* of learning rather than collecting points and rubric scores to cash in for grades. Descriptive rubrics as opposed to evaluative rubrics [see Figure 5.8] keep

| | Descriptive rubrics | Evaluative rubrics |
|---|---|---|
| **Answer this question for students →** | *How much of the task did you complete?* | *How well did you complete the task?* |
| **Definition** | Spells out the *work* of a particular task with the different aspects of the task students need to do in order for the task to be considered complete. | Articulates the *skills* and *content knowledge* to be demonstrated via a task with different levels of achievement for different categories, all boiled down to an overall score. |
| **Format** | Essentially the instructions of the task in rubric or checklist form. | Varies—but often a table/grid with criteria and levels of achievement for each criterion. |
| **Written by** | Teachers, students | Teachers, students, external entities (AP, IB, school district, etc.) |
| **Used by** | Teachers: to quickly communicate to students if they are finished with a particular task.<br><br>Students: to check to be sure they've taken care of all aspects of a given task and to determine what to work on if a task is only partially complete. | Students: to self-evaluate their own or evaluate their peers' work.<br><br>Teachers: to determine instructional moves based on how students are doing toward the different categories on the rubric.<br><br>External entities: to evaluate student work in more high-stakes situations. |

Figure 5.8 Descriptive Rubrics vs. Evaluative Rubrics
The key distinctions between descriptive and evaluative rubrics.

a vision of what the work of learning looks like at the center of the classroom, putting students in the driver's seat. They don't have to guess. They know what they can do to get there.

Using rubric scores to determine high-stakes grades makes it possible to rate and rank some language uses over others, thereby perpetuating societal structures that oppress and marginalize individuals. Asao Inoue argues that any writing rubric we have is likely couched in a white racial framework of language use (2015, 2020). When one way of using language dominates, it is difficult to see the sophistication in *all* of our students' language use, enacting white language supremacy. Moving away from the ranking and sorting made possible by rubrics in traditional grading is one place we can stop blindly participating in systemic racism.

### *Invite Students to Help You Keep Track of Whether They're Doing the Work or Not*

Students can't actually enter their own completion data into the gradebook, but they can complete tasks that might make *our* data entry more efficient. For example, students could check off on a list, one by one, which of the week's tasks they completed. This is an effective self-reflection moment for students, *and* we can use their resulting answers as a weekly data point in the gradebook.

I have a gradebook category called "the doing of the work." It contains one assignment each week worth as many points as there were tasks for that week. If there were five tasks, the week's "doing of the work" assignment is worth 5 points, and I record the number of tasks each student completed. I compare students' self-reported numbers on the weekly check-in with my own records on the rosters on my clipboard to make sure we're on the same page.

I've had students who only turn in work once I mark it missing in the gradebook. I've found this weekly checklist helps those students become more proactive about keeping up with their work. The overall percentage for "the doing of the work" indicates how many of the course's tasks students complete within the weeks they are due, telling students if they are engaging with the class consistently, participating earnestly, truly present along the way. It becomes a reminder to students about something—within their control—they can focus on to positively impact their learning.

## Assessment *Data Sources* for CP10 Learning Goals

| Learning Goal ⇩ | Your work to examine | Assessment data in LMS/Gradebook |
|---|---|---|
| **ONE:** Consider an author's choices as you read to figure out what YOU think a text means overall. | OTAs, rambling thoughts, weekly writing (if it's about the reading), what you say in class conversations (whole-class and small group) | Reading comprehension pre/interim/post assessment scores, reading comprehension check scores, completion of reading tasks, reading conference notes, notes on reading tasks |
| **TWO:** Examine individual words closely to derive meaning in a text. | | |
| **THREE:** Write narratives, arguments, and informative pieces, effectively saying what you think about topics that matter to you. | Weekly writing, writer's memos | Completion of revision tasks, rubric scores, writing conference notes, notes on writing tasks |
| **FOUR:** Revise extensively to improve a piece of writing. | Revision work, writer's memos | |
| **FIVE:** Engage in meaningful conversation with others to figure out what YOU think. | What you say in class conversations (whole-class and small group) | Participation in whole-class conversations, notes on speaking tasks |
| **SIX:** Successfully speak aloud your ideas to class. | What you say in class conversations (whole-class and small group), presentations, what you say if ever invited to speak aloud | How often you choose to speak in whole-class conversations, notes on speaking tasks |
| **SEVEN:** Gather and use information from a variety of sources to develop and support your ideas. | Weekly writing, the citation tool in Google Docs | Notes on writing tasks, conference notes |
| **EIGHT:** Demonstrate successful student habits. | Your own reflections about how well you're paying attention, getting work done, staying focused, stashing your phone every day, bringing your laptop every day, always having your writer's notebook, regularly checking LMS/gradebook, etc. | Completed work percentage, late work flags, attendance/tardies |
| **NINE:** Practice effective self-reflection, self-evaluation, and metacognition. | Your own reflections about how well you're paying attention to your learning goals and monitoring progress, learning goal OTAs | Learning goal self-evaluations, notes on reflection tasks, conference notes |
| **TEN:** Be a positive community member. | Your own reflection on feedback you give others, how well you encourage your group to be focused, how well you lift up others in class, your contributions in shared digital spaces, etc. | Attendance/tardies, notes on various tasks, conference notes |

**Figure 5.9** Classroom Assessment Data Sources for the Tenth-Grade Learning Goals

## Help Students *See* Their Own Progress Toward Their Learning Goals

Just asking students to reflect (via the strategies earlier in this chapter) is only half of it; they need meaningful assessment data to reflect upon. Our classrooms must produce assessment data relevant to all of the learning goals. Figure 5.9 is a document that outlines assessment data sources for the tenth-grade learning goals from earlier in this chapter.

I ask students to highlight or circle the assessment data sources they think will help them to track their progress on the learning goals they've set for themselves. I invite them to share what they've selected with their table group, including any ideas they have about additional data sources they might track as well. Every bit of conversation puts *student* use of classroom assessment data at the center. With this document and the brief conversation about it, students will know where they can look for relevant evidence and moments when they reflect on their learning goal progress each week.

Students can also see their growth and progress toward their learning goals by revisiting the learning progressions to self-evaluate again. I invited Kai and his classmates to reevaluate using the learning progressions toward the end of the semester as they were preparing to write their semester grade letters and select their final grades. By reevaluating and then comparing their results to their self-evaluation from the beginning of the semester, students can look for growth toward their goals.

Figure 5.10 is Kai's September self-evaluation on the learning progression for goal #1, what he based his first personal goal on in his plan for learning and growth.

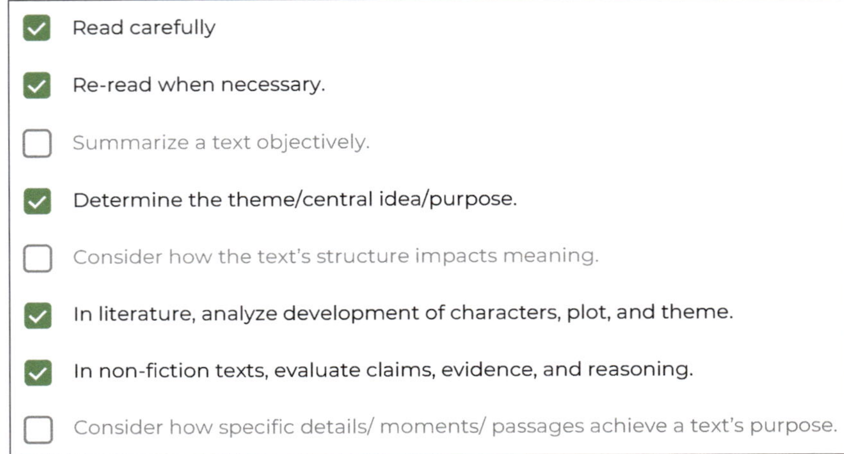

- [x] Read carefully
- [x] Re-read when necessary.
- [ ] Summarize a text objectively.
- [x] Determine the theme/central idea/purpose.
- [ ] Consider how the text's structure impacts meaning.
- [x] In literature, analyze development of characters, plot, and theme.
- [x] In non-fiction texts, evaluate claims, evidence, and reasoning.
- [ ] Consider how specific details/ moments/ passages achieve a text's purpose.

**Figure 5.10** Kai's September Self-Evaluation on the Learning Progression for Goal #1

Figure 5.11 is Kai's selfreevaluation in December.

- [x] Read carefully
- [x] Re-read when necessary.
- [x] Summarize a text objectively.
- [ ] Determine the theme/central idea/purpose.
- [ ] Consider how the text's structure impacts meaning.
- [x] In literature, analyze development of characters, plot, and theme.
- [x] In non-fiction texts, evaluate claims, evidence, and reasoning.
- [x] Consider how specific details/ moments/ passages achieve a text's purpose.

**Figure 5.11** Kai's December Self-Evaluation on the Learning Progression for Goal #1

In December, Kai was able to check off the final box in the learning progression—meaning that he felt confident he could achieve what that item describes. Considering he used that learning progression step to narrow and focus his personal learning goal for reading, being able to check it off shows he has made progress in this goal. The differences in the check boxes for some earlier items in the progression between Kai's September and December self-evaluations give him some things to think about and reflect upon as he approaches writing about his journey toward this learning goal.

## Provide Clear Guidelines for Final Grade Selection

Anxieties students (or their parents!) have about the non-traditional grading in my class usually surround potential disagreement at semester's end. Students worry that they'll select an A but I might disagree and at the last minute they end up with a D. From early on in a term, it's important that students understand what it means to be able to select the grade they are hoping for by the end of the term.

My grade guidelines come in two formats. One is a general page of descriptors for each grade level [see Figure 5.12]. About the time students see the learning goals for the class (five or so weeks into the school year), they also get these grade descriptions. I want students to know that because their final grade isn't simply a matter of collecting enough points,

**Grade Descriptions**

To get credit for the semester, no assignments in the "major tasks" category can be missing. For this semester, those major tasks include:

- Plan for learning and growth
- Culminating unit tasks
- Final exam task(s)
- Semester grade letter/story

**A** = You met deadlines (goal 8), followed instructions (goal 8), were a positive community member (goal 9), and collected evidence of compelling growth (goal 10) toward your learning objectives. The story in your letter fully explains and shows that growth—with specific detail—toward each of your chosen learning goals. Your completed work percentage is in the high 90s with no missing weekly writing tasks, no more than one or two missed minor tasks and all major tasks "complete."

**B** = You did the work well, but there were a few things you could have done more with, or you could have been better with due dates and following instructions, or you could have been a more positive community member. You have clear evidence of growth, but it is not as compelling perhaps as it could be, or the story in your letter does not explain/show your growth as fully or as detailed as it could.

**C** = You did work, but there were several things you could have done more with. You don't have as much evidence of growth toward your learning objectives as you could have, or the story in your letter explains/shows your growth minimally.

**D** = You did minimal work and have minimal evidence of growth toward your learning objectives. There was a lot that you could have done much better.

**F** = You did not turn in one or more of the major assignments for the class.

***NOTE:*** *You cannot be knocked out of a particular grade category for one little thing.*

**Figure 5.12** Grade Descriptions

there has to be a baseline for what it takes, minimally, to get credit for the class. The very first item on the document makes it clear that to get credit for the class, no major tasks can be missing. They don't have to be fully complete—they just can't be missing.

The rest of the document offers a general description for each letter grade and a caveat at the end: "You cannot be knocked out of a particular grade category for one little thing. That would be silly." I added this disclaimer a few years ago when students worried that even one late assignment would mean the difference between an A and a B.

My grade descriptions are a result of conversations with students over the years. I do not re-negotiate them every year with each new group of students like I thought I would when I began my non-traditional grading adventure years ago. I tried to in those first few years, but it takes a lot of time. Students told me they felt betrayed: for a class that promised to sidestep the traditional grading game, there we were talking at length about grades. To save that time and to keep the class air time about grades to a minimum, I present the grade descriptions, explain to students where they came from, and invite them to suggest refinements.

The second format of the grade guidelines [Figure 5.13] is a checklist version to help students consider what each aspect of the grade descriptions means for their grade selection.

The note in the bottom right of the table indicates that this is not a set-in-stone rubric to determine a student's final grade. Instead, it's a starting place. As students check off the items in each row that best describe their data, they create a visual that helps them think about which grade category best lines up with their work.

It would be unfair for students to see these two documents only at the end of the semester, past the point where they could adjust their route to get to the grade they are hoping to select. Every time we have to post a progress grade (in my school we do this mid-way through each semester) is an opportunity for students to self-evaluate on the grade descriptions

## Grade Descriptions Checklist

| Data to consider | For an A | For a B | For a C | For a D | For an F |
|---|---|---|---|---|---|
| Tasks in the "can't be missing to get credit for the class" category in the gradebook | ☐ None are missing.<br>☐ All are complete.<br>☐ None are late. | ☐ I'm between A and C. | ☐ None are missing.<br>☐ More than one task is not "complete."<br>☐ More than one task is late. | ☐ I can't check off what it says for a C. | ☐ At least one major task is missing. |
| Growth on your three learning goals, as you will describe them in your semester grade letter/story | ☐ I can describe significant growth on all three of my learning goals in specific detail. | ☐ I'm between A and C. | ☐ I only have some growth I can describe toward my three goals, and/or I have minimal detail. | ☐ I can't check off what it says for a C. | ***NOTE: Use this checklist as a general starting point for your grade selection. There's room here to consider unique student stories.*** |
| Overall gradebook percentage *(represents how completely you did the work–not just how many tasks, but how completely you did what each tasked asked)* | ☐ High 90s | ☐ I'm between A and C. | ☐ 70s to low 80s | ☐ I can't check off what it says for a C. | |
| Tasks in the "weekly writing" category in the gradebook | ☐ None are missing.<br>☐ All are complete.<br>☐ Two or fewer are late. | ☐ I'm between A and C. | ☐ More than 2-3 tasks are missing or "cannot"<br>☐ Several tasks are late. | ☐ I can't check off what it says for a C. | |
| Totals in the "the doing of the work" category. *(The points possible is the total # of tasks for the semester. The score is how many of them you completed within the week they were due.)* | ☐ My score is within 7 or so of the total points possible. | ☐ I'm between A and C. | ☐ My score is more than 7 or so away from the total points possible, but I completed most. | ☐ I can't check off what it says for a C. | |

Figure 5.13 Grade Descriptions Checklist

and reflect on what they want to improve in the time ahead. The grade descriptions checklist is also a meaningful artifact to put at the center of quick check-in conferences with students or even conferences with parents.

You may be wondering what to do when students choose a grade that doesn't line up with the grade descriptions. This actually happens far less than you might imagine. With clear grade guidelines that students see and work with well ahead of grade selection time, most self-evaluate fairly. But when they don't, I offer them a path to still get there. For example, I might write back to a student, "Your letter doesn't quite yet describe your growth toward your goals in as much detail as it could. I'll put in a B for now, but I invite you to revisit the sample grade letters from past students, revise your letter, and resubmit." Or, "The grade descriptions do indicate that all of the major tasks should be complete for an A. You have one that's not quite there yet. I invite you to complete it before we finalize your semester grade. Let me know how I can help." Or (my favorite), "When I look across the grade descriptions and think about your work, it seems that you can check off more in the A column than you did. Is it okay with you if I put in an A instead of a B?"

A final note about language here. I am deliberate with the word "select." I don't want students "arguing" for their grades or "proving" their case or saying what grade they "earned." Those words emphasize the power dynamic involved in traditional grading. My students can't *actually* put in their own grades. I have to do that. And technically I could override the grades they choose. The power dynamic does exist. But we can minimize it, removing ourselves from the center of the grading process and finding places for our students to drive instead. Language matters. "Selecting" the grade that "captures the work you did" is a much different task than "arguing" for the grade you think you "earned." The former is a task that cultivates student agency; the latter positions the teacher as the gatekeeper, a person they have to convince to agree on a letter grade. This is why I don't respond to students by saying I "agree" with their selection. "I'll put in an A," for example, is the language I use.

## The Most Valuable Part of the Process: The Final Grade Letter/Story

The strategies in this chapter set students up to look back over their growth and write the story of their journey as learners. In examining their

**Dear students,**

Please write a letter in which you

- Tell the story of the journey you've taken for each of your learning goals.
    - Where did you start?
    - Where did you end up?
    - What happened along the way?
- Consider where you struggled.
    - Where along your journey in particular did you struggle?
    - How much of that struggle was in your locus of control?
    - What else was going on that created the struggle?
- Celebrate your successes.
- Select the letter grade that best captures your journey according to our grade descriptions.

**Figure 5.14** Semester Grade Letter/Story Invitation

collection of weekly learning goal moments, they discover where they started with each goal, where they ended up, and what happened along the way. I ask for a story because it is how we humans make sense of everything (Newkirk, 2014). Using story deliberately as a frame to understand something helps us to know it well. I hope that by writing about their learning as a story, my students will know clearly the paths they took.

The invitation I extend at semester's end for the grade letter is in Figure 5.14. Let's look at an excerpt from Kai's grade letter/story:

> Going into my learning goals, I put down "breaking down a text's purpose". When we were in the Antigone unit, I was able to practice this heavily. I took advantage of the OTA strategy that you've taught the class, which benefited me to grow in that area. Many of the exercises we did in class helped with the goal as well. For instance, the tournament bracket of who suffered the most in Antigone was an awesome way to break down the purpose of it all. At the start of the semester, I was able to determine the theme of texts, but not go deeper into detail.
>
> My next goal was to summarize agreement/disagreement in a discussion. This one came easier to me, because I feel like I'm best at class discussions and speaking aloud. When I was in the circle discussion with classmates, I made an effort to do this, although part of me felt like I had already given my opinion and people knew my thoughts. I'm going to try to continue with this goal into next semester. I hope we'll do more class discussions so I can improve.

> Something that helped me improve and become confident with my writing was just trusting myself and believing that my ideas are valid. That happened to also be my third semester goal. The weekly writings where I could write about what I wanted helped me. Every week it felt like I got a bit better, and writing was coming more naturally. On my latest assignment I wrote about The Beatles and how their song "Let It Be" has meant so much to me. On this assignment I felt this goal really kicked in, I wasn't overthinking it at all, and I was able to recognize that I've really improved in that area.

Because Kai included specific detail about each of his goals that helped me to see the learning journey he had traversed, and because he had done the work of the class (mostly on time but not always), it made sense that he was "deciding to select an A for [him]self this semester," as he wrote at the start of his letter. Kai's growth is clear—to me by reading what he has written and (more importantly) to him. That's the entire point. By writing the *story* of his learning, Kai can see clearly—for himself—what he has learned.

Every semester when I read students' letters, their insight about their own learning reminds me how critical this task is. But reading their letters and responding takes time. So I ask for their letters by the Friday before finals week and design engaging and interactive culminating tasks during the final exam blocks that produce no stacks of student work for me to deal with after—like a structured whole-class conversation or something similar. This reserves time during finals week to read grade letters, write students back, and engage in additional conversation with them as needed.

## The Goal Is Independence

Just like with the reading, writing, and talk strategies of the previous chapters, we can use grading and assessment strategies that keep students out front, doing the most important thinking and work. As a quick summary review of the strategies in this chapter, Figure 5.15 shows how the Three Step Meaning Making Process organizes strategies that will keep us out of students' way as they drive their own grading and assessment.

It's critical a learner's overall grade doesn't hinge on evaluation, on constant point collecting, on a percentage that changes by the minute creating a high-stress atmosphere where the teacher has all the control.

<table>
<tr><th colspan="2">Meaning Making process step</th><th>Strategies for goal setting</th><th>Strategies for progress monitoring</th></tr>
<tr><td>ONE:</td><td>• What do you notice about yourself as a learner?</td><td>Self -evaluate on learning progressions for course learning goals.<br>*The teacher needs to craft a clear set of learning goals and sketch out learning progressions for those go als.</td><td>Reflect weekly on progress (OTAs or learning goal moments)<br>*The teacher needs to make sure the classroom produces assessment data students can use to reflect on their progress.</td></tr>
<tr><td rowspan="2">TWO:</td><td rowspan="2">• What do you want to improve on in the time ahead?<br>• Where are you growing? Where are you not growing?</td><td>Examine assessment data sources to determine to what to work on.</td><td>Self-evaluate toward grade guidelines and choose areas to improve in the time ahead.</td></tr>
<tr><td colspan="2">*The teacher needs to make sure the classroom produces assessment data students can use to help with goal setting and progress monitoring.<br>*The teacher needs to help students see if they are doing the work or not.</td></tr>
<tr><td>THREE:</td><td>• What do you want to learn? (at the start of the term)<br>• What have you learned? (at the end of the term)</td><td>Craft a plan for learning and growth.</td><td>Re-evaluate using learning progressions for course learning goals to determine growth.<br>Write the story of the learning journey.<br>*The teacher needs to provide clear grade descriptions to support student grade selection.</td></tr>
</table>

**Figure 5.15** Three Step Meaning Making Process for Grading Strategies

Design a path to the grade where students drive, that is most meaningful for them first, and that they have control over, so they know exactly what they need to do to learn.

Of course, it's perfectly acceptable to generate some traditional assessment data. But I encourage you to keep it in perspective. We don't have to calculate quantitative assessment data into an overall final grade just because that's what the traditional grading system expects. Instead, we can invite students to use assessment data to track their own learning.

What does or should a final grade represent anyhow? Mastery? Growth? Work ethic? Eligibility to compete in sports? Ability to succeed in college? Workplace readiness? Level of preparation for the next class? Qualification for car insurance discounts? The truth is there are audiences of our students' grades (often via our students' transcripts) who will read them for some or all of those purposes. We can't possibly produce a single data point that will capture everything for each of those purposes. I'm not saying we should dismiss those purposes. I just want each of my students, first and foremost, to know what their final grade represents. I want them to look at it and remember the meaningful learning journey they traveled, centering on the growth they achieved along the way.

Why are we so hung up on grades anyhow? Why are we so focused on making sure they are fair and accurate? Why do we care what they represent to other people? Why are we so careful to make sure students aren't getting As unless they really truly deserve them? Whose rules are *we* playing by when we play that role? Which oppressive societal systems are we perpetuating?

What changes in your classroom if you think of your students as the primary users of assessment data so they can use it to set their own goals, make their own plan for growth, and monitor the learning journey they travel?

Shifting the primary purpose of assessment data in my classroom changed everything. For the better.

Whenever someone pushes back at more humanizing grading practices because they're more comfortable with the traditional grading system or have fears about stepping out of the driver's seat, my thoughts circle back to Alfie Kohn's words:

> If we begin with a desire to assess more often, or to produce more data, or to improve the consistency of our grading, then certain prescriptions will follow. If, however, our point of departure isn't mostly about the grading, but about our desire for students to understand ideas from the inside out, or to get a kick out of playing with words and numbers, or to be in charge of their own learning, then we will likely end up elsewhere. We may come to see grading as a huge, noisy, fuel-guzzling, smoke-belching machine that constantly requires repairs and new parts, when what we should be doing is pulling the plug.
>
> *(Kohn, 2011)*

CHAPTER 6

# DESIGN THE CLASSROOM SPACE TO SUPPORT STUDENT-DRIVEN LEARNING

> Dear Doctor Zerwin,
>
> At the beginning of the semester, the problems didn't necessarily lie in how much I was writing or even how nice it sounded; the issue was with how I was thinking, how I chose what to write about, and the things I was scared of.

Emily's semester grade letter/story articulates how her ability to develop her *own* thinking about the texts in eleventh- grade International Baccalaureate Literature grew over the course of the semester. Before she joined the class, Emily had honed her process to figure out something to write about books. It was a safe process that ensured she would get the grade she wanted without having to think through ideas that she wasn't entirely sure of.

> In past years, basic analysis of books had come somewhat easily to me, but I was starting to develop an approach to analyzing texts that was much too formulaic. I think that often, I was running everything I read through the same processor in my brain and using the same basic system to do all of my writing work. The system worked something like this:
>
> Read book. Write a lot in book. Think about book. Find something you feel like you understand really well? Good. Write a lot

> about that. Not confident about your idea? See if first page of internet search results seems to agree with you. If not, consider backtracking. Concept or motif that you don't understand? System error. Avoid those concepts. Stick to what you understand. Writing about what you're not confused about = better grade.
>
> This system works if you want to get a decent grade, but it's like looking at a book with tunnel vision. It's learning to write for a grade, not learning how to think. If a writing assignment had a giant ugly grade attached to it, of course I was going to write about something I felt like I understood. If I leaned into things I was confused about, there was always the risk that I wouldn't figure anything out and then my grade would suffer.

Because of the grading practices explored in Chapter 5 that removed any "giant ugly grade[s]" looming over her writing, Emily became less intimidated about confronting what she found confusing about literature. Let's jump ahead to Emily's description of her meaning making toward the end of the semester:

> When we started *The Stranger* [(Camus, 1989)], anything that was left of the mental processor got completely blown up. It was impossible to only focus on things I understood because for a while, I was confused about almost everything that was happening. All of my OTAs had questions on them. My rambling thoughts were full of questions, and so were my Harkness notes. I tried to answer as many as I could by rambling and by collecting my thoughts in my notebook after Harkness discussions. As I worked through my questions, I went from utter confusion about the book to feeling like I'd gained a much better understanding of what Camus was trying to tell us with this work. I started to realize that with certain books, it's simply not possible to figure everything out before you start writing, and if I hadn't asked so many questions or explored things I was confused about, I wouldn't have gotten much out of the story.

Emily describes how she worked through her growing list of questions about *The Stranger* in original thought annotations (OTAs) and Rambling Thoughts (see Chapter 2) and through her notes and writing about class Harkness discussions. Putting these three key components of the class on

repeat every week gave Emily the space to build the skills she needed to grow from "utter confusion" to what *she* thought Camus was trying to say with the book.

> At the beginning of the semester, I wrote in my first letter to you, "it's very hard for me to sit down and write something without having it all planned out in my head first, without knowing how it will end, without knowing how to make it meaningful, without it being perfect." Every year that I have to talk about things I struggle with and set goals for myself in LA, I say that I struggle with being a perfectionist and that I want to loosen up, take more risks, and be okay with not always knowing things. And every year, things only get worse. That's what I expected to happen this year, but it didn't. Instead, I became more comfortable writing about things I didn't fully understand, I asked more questions, and I got better at looking through perspectives different from my own. I learned to be okay with not knowing things and figuring them out during my writing process, I loosened my expectations of trying to produce things as close to perfection as I could, and I learned how to take risks so that I could think about things in depth and develop ideas about concepts that I didn't feel like I had a clue about. I've conquered anxieties and struggles to change my approach to writing and thinking for the better.

We only have so much time in class with our students each week. We have to plan carefully to protect time and space for the student-driven practices this book describes. Our students will learn to value what we spend our precious class time on. This chapter offers ways to think about how to design our classroom space for student-driven learning where students will practice and value their *own* meaning making: a predictable weekly routine that protects time for the most important work, helping students feel safe in the classroom community, and co-creating the classroom space with students.

## Scheduling Time Behind the Wheel with a Predictable Weekly Routine

We obviously teach both reading and writing. But some curricula place reading at the forefront over writing, and some emphasize writing first.

For example, the curriculum expectations for Emily's IB Literature class make it clear that the course is about the study and analysis of literature. It's a *reading* class that uses writing to support literary analytic thinking. Primarily, all of the IB assessments are about literary analysis. This understanding should drive the design of class routines that protect time for students to use student-driven reading, writing, and talk strategies to grow their abilities to make their own meaning from literary texts.

Not all curricula are so laser focused on literary analysis. Recall Kai's goal setting and reflection in Chapter 5. The curriculum for his on-grade-level tenth-grade class requires students to read a range of texts and to write for a range of purposes. Freed from a narrower focus on literary analysis, the class has wider possibilities. To rein these in, I consider writing the primary focus for the class. Kai and his classmates read, yes, but all for the purpose of giving them things to write about and to study moves of other writers they can attempt in their own writing. Given these clear priorities, the class's weekly routine can protect time for students to use student-driven reading, writing, and talk strategies to grow their abilities to develop their own voice as writers.

Figure 6.1 explores how a course's primary focus—writing or reading—impacts how we might organize the strategies in this book into a weekly routine. It's not impossible to plan a weekly routine that weighs reading and writing equally. Or perhaps to plan a course so that you spend a few weeks with a routine that puts writing at the forefront and then a few weeks with a routine that puts reading at the forefront. The challenge, though, with the nature of our curriculum is that it's endless. We will never be able to include everything possible in the time we have. Without a clear, narrow focus, we may attempt to stuff our weeks with more than our students can possibly accomplish successfully—at least that has been my own personal experience. Without a clear, narrow focus, students will struggle to know the *why* behind the work. Less is more. Both for our students and for us.

So keep it simple. Invite students to practice the same strategies over and over. Put them on repeat until students internalize the work. A predictable weekly routine establishes boundaries around the time your students have in your classroom, communicates what the work is that they'll do in the space, and assures them you've designed the classroom deliberately so they can come to it, do work that matters to them, and grow in ways that will help them for the rest of their lives.

| | Writing-focused class | Reading-focused class |
|---|---|---|
| **Overall goal** | Build writer's voices | Build readers' own theories about texts |
| **Put these things on repeat week by week** | Weekly writing with a small Revision task (Step 1: *Start Small* and Step 2: *Seek Connections*) | OTAs, Rambling Thoughts, class discussion (Step 1: *Start Small* and Step 2: *Seek Connections*) |
| **Every few weeks, break the routine to** | Polish up a piece of writing to include in a portfolio of work (Step 3: *Take Action*) | Articulate overall ideas about a text through writing or speaking (Step 3: *Take Action*) |
| **Purpose of reading tasks** | To support and inspire writing. | To practice and build confidence in making sense of complex texts. |
| **Purpose of writing tasks** | To practice and build writing confidence. | To discover one's own thinking about complex texts and to communicate ideas figured out. |
| **Purpose of classroom talk** | ➔ Reader feedback (Step 2: *Seek Connections*)<br>➔ Discussion of shared texts to inspire ideas for what to write about (Step 2: *Seek Connections*) | ➔ Discussion of shared texts to try out and build ideas (Step 2: *Seek Connections*) |
| **Purpose of ongoing student self-reflection** | How students are progressing on the journeys they planned for themselves with their plans for learning and growth. | |

**Figure 6.1** Considerations for a Writing-Focused vs. a Reading-Focused Class

A note on "weekly"—depending on the needs of your particular class, you may need to spread the same tasks you'll see in the following weekly routines over two or maybe even three weeks. The weekly routine in this chapter for a reading-centered class is essentially the weekly routine for Emily's IB Literature course. It's the right routine for her and her classmates. But for our on-grade-level classes, my colleagues and I are feeling the need to slow down. We're experimenting with a two-week or even three-week version of the weekly routine for a writing-centered class you'll read about next.

Think carefully about the needs of your particular students. Would they need more time than a week to really sink into the work outlined below? If so, what might the best regular routine—anchored on the Three Step Meaning Making Process—look like for *your* students?

### *An Example Weekly Routine for a Writing-Centered Class*

If our primary objective is to help students build their voice as writers, they need to write a lot, far more than we can ever hope to read and respond to. We just don't have to look at every word they write. Inviting lots of rough notebook writing that we'll never look at gives students a safe place to practice getting lots of words on the page.

We don't have to look at every word they write, but we *do* need to look at enough of their writing to inform our next instructional moves. A weekly piece of writing that's a bit more formal than notebook writing yet not a finalized draft provides the volume we need to inform instruction and that students need to grow as writers.

In Figure 6.3, notice that the example weekly routine is heavily focused on what the *students* are doing during class. Most of the class time each day is for students to *do* the work embedded in the Three Step Meaning Making Process. Yes, of course, there are times when we'll need to step in with some quick instruction. We can do that with brief mini lessons or brief mini lectures, but it's critical we do not let moments where we are talking eat up students' time to work and build meaning on their own.

This example includes daily reading time because a few minutes of silent reading to start each class settles students into the space and gets words in their head to contextualize and inspire the writing work the weekly routine supports. Students use the daily reading time for the current reading focus: a whole-class text, reading in book clubs, independent reading, or shared short texts relevant to the writing work that week.

Every few weeks, the routine varies a bit to give students space to polish some writing more fully. They read each piece they wrote over the previous weeks. They choose the writing they most want to improve, perhaps based on what they said in their writer's memo about what they would do next if they kept working on a particular piece. For example, after several weeks of experimenting with memoir writing alongside reading Satrapi's (2004) *Persepolis*, my sophomores used the revision week to either combine the memoir writing they had done each week or to select one individual piece they wanted to develop more fully. And looking over several weeks' worth of their attempts at memoir writing gave me ideas for mini lessons I could offer during that revision week to help them grow as memoirists.

Figure 6.4 shows what the week looks like when students are doing that more extended revision.

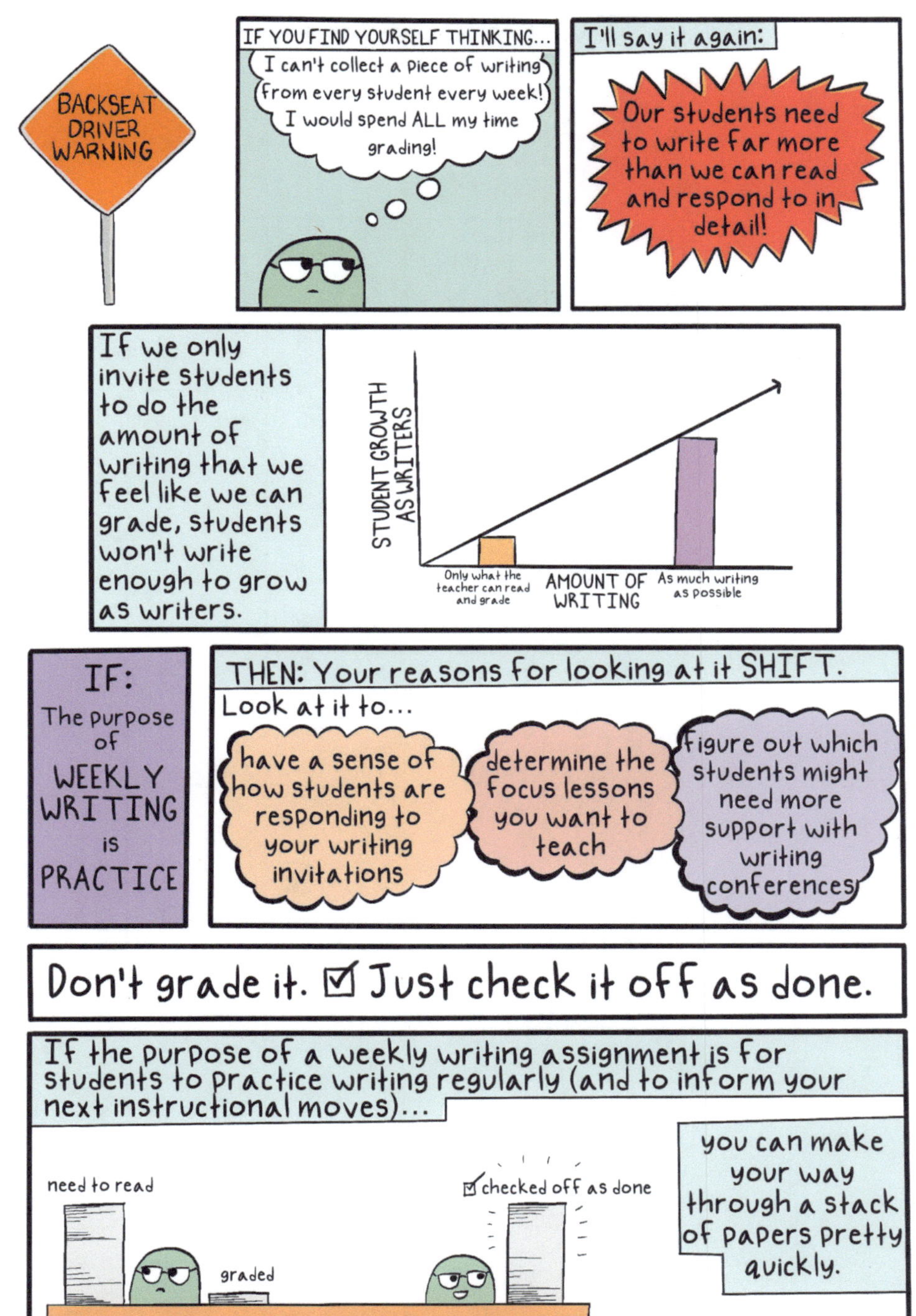


**Figure 6.2** Backseat Driver Warning

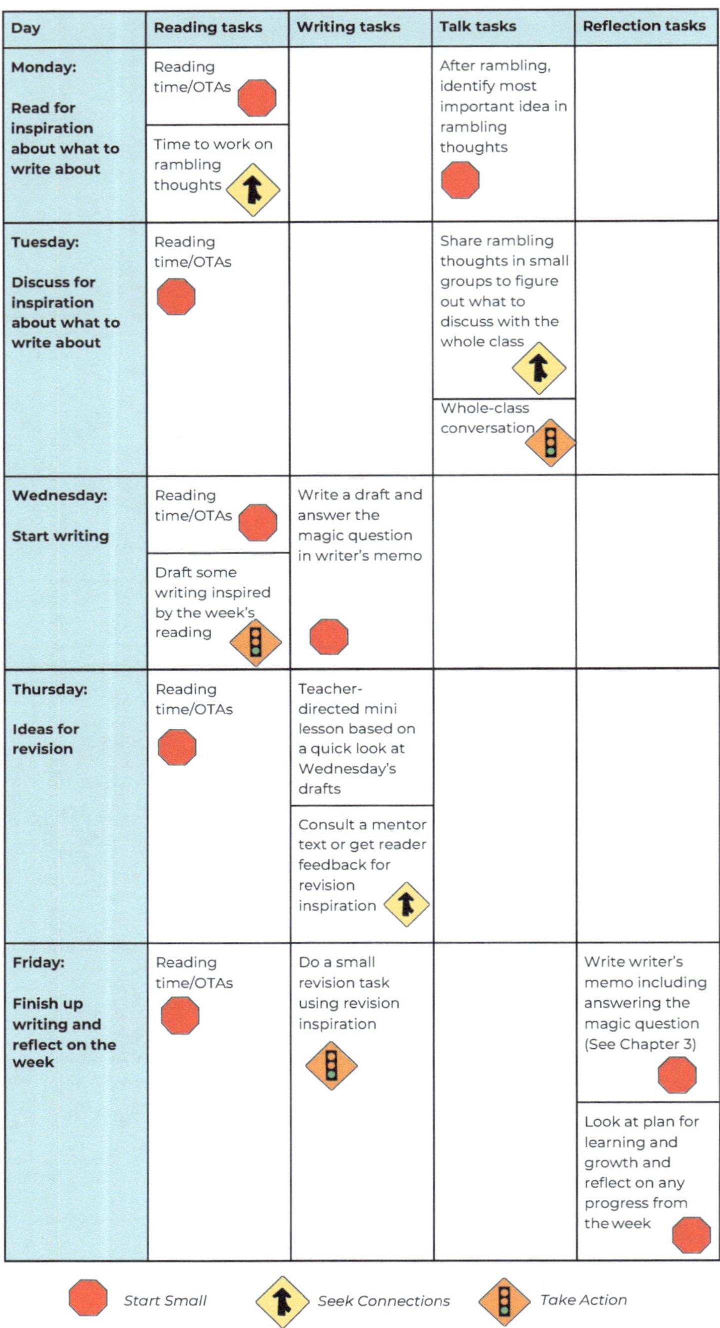

| Day | Reading tasks | Writing tasks | Talk tasks | Reflection tasks |
|---|---|---|---|---|
| **Monday:**<br><br>**Read for inspiration about what to write about** | Reading time/OTAs<br><br>Time to work on rambling thoughts | | After rambling, identify most important idea in rambling thoughts | |
| **Tuesday:**<br><br>**Discuss for inspiration about what to write about** | Reading time/OTAs | | Share rambling thoughts in small groups to figure out what to discuss with the whole class<br><br>Whole-class conversation | |
| **Wednesday:**<br><br>**Start writing** | Reading time/OTAs<br><br>Draft some writing inspired by the week's reading | Write a draft and answer the magic question in writer's memo | | |
| **Thursday:**<br><br>**Ideas for revision** | Reading time/OTAs | Teacher-directed mini lesson based on a quick look at Wednesday's drafts<br><br>Consult a mentor text or get reader feedback for revision inspiration | | |
| **Friday:**<br><br>**Finish up writing and reflect on the week** | Reading time/OTAs | Do a small revision task using revision inspiration | | Write writer's memo including answering the magic question (See Chapter 3)<br><br>Look at plan for learning and growth and reflect on any progress from the week |

*Start Small* *Seek Connections* *Take Action*

**Figure 6.3** Example Weekly Routine That Forefronts Writing

| Day | Reading tasks | Writing tasks | Talk tasks | Reflection tasks |
|---|---|---|---|---|
| **Monday:** | Reading time/OTAs | Time to look over previous week's drafts and writer's memos to identify which writing to revise/develop more fully | | |
| **Tuesday:** | Reading time/OTAs | Teacher-directed mini lesson based on observations about previous weeks' writing. | Using the mini-lesson as a focus, talk in small groups about the pieces identified on Monday and what they might focus on in revision | |
| **Wednesday:** | Reading time/OTAs | Workshop one student's piece of writing as a class on a shared display. (See Chapter 4 for more about whole-class workshop) | | |
| | | Students start revising their own writing | | |
| **Thursday:** | Reading time/OTAs | Teacher-directed mini lesson on some aspect of mechanics for students to focus on as they polish their writing. | | |
| | | Time for revising | | |
| **Friday:** | Reading time/OTAs | Time for revising | | Write revision memo to describe the work done in revision |
| | | | | Look at plan for learning and growth and reflect on any progress from the week |

*Start Small* *Seek Connections* *Take Action*

**Figure 6.4** Revision Week Routine

The Tuesday teacher-directed mini lesson could be a brief look at a mentor text (perhaps one that students read during reading time that day). Or it could include the teacher sharing some of their own process, like I did one year with my own bit of memoir writing as I described in Chapter 3. I realized I was not actually writing a story, a similar issue I saw across many students' memoir pieces, so I shared with them a strategy I used myself to add more narrative elements to my writing. The Thursday teacher-directed mini lesson could focus more on mechanics since students are polishing a piece of writing. The mini lesson should reflect common mechanical errors in students' writing as a whole. And remember, these teacher-directed moments are *mini* lessons. Set a timer for ten minutes and stick to it. Students need time to revise!

A predictable, weekly routine anchored on student-driven writing protects time for students to practice—again and again—strategies that grow their voices as writers.

### An Example Weekly Routine for a Reading-Centered Class

If our primary objective is to support students as they build their own theories about complex texts, they need a lot of practice starting with their own initial ideas about texts and building thinking from there. A weekly routine that puts that cycle on repeat, week by week, provides the time and space to do that important practice [see Figure 6.5].

| Day | Reading tasks | Writing tasks | Talk tasks | Reflection tasks |
|---|---|---|---|---|
| **Monday:**<br><br>**Read text(s), notice what you notice on your own, start building your thinking.** | Reading time/OTAs<br><br>Time to work on rambling thoughts | | | |
| **Tuesday:**<br><br>**Read text(s), share thinking about text(s) in small groups to prepare for whole-class conversation.** | Reading time/OTAs | | Identify most important idea in rambling thoughts<br><br>Share those important ideas in small groups to figure out what to discuss with the whole class | |
| **Wednesday:**<br><br>**Discuss text(s) with the whole class.** | Reading time/OTAs | | Whole class conversation | |
| **Thursday:**<br><br>**Read text(s) and think about how you might eventually communicate what you're figuring out about the text(s).** | Reading time/OTAs | Teacher-directed instruction to help students capture what from the week they might want to explore in the eventual writing they'll do about the text. | | |
| **Friday:**<br><br>**Read text(s) and reflect on the week.** | Reading time/OTAs | | | Look at plan for learning and growth and reflect on any progress from the week |

*Start Small* *Seek Connections* *Take Action*

**Figure 6.5** Example Weekly Routine That Forefronts Reading

You'll notice there are some items in this weekly routine that are the same in the weekly routine that forefronts writing. Students read and complete OTAs every day, and they reflect on their personal learning goals every Friday. But this routine protects more time for classroom talk tasks that support students as they build their thinking about the reading. And there could be more time for a longer daily reading time—fifteen or twenty minutes instead of ten. There could even be time for most of a class period one day for reading to support students in getting the reading done. Remember, we show students what matters most by what we spend time on in class. If reading matters, we should dedicate class time to it. Ample independent reading time also gives us space for one-on-one reading instruction in conferences.

Every few weeks, a break in the routine provides an opportunity for students to move on to the "take action" step with the reading strategies. The needs of the specific curriculum help to determine what the "take action" step should be. In Emily's eleventh-grade IB Literature class, they write several drafts of the essay they'll eventually submit to IB as an external assessment. So after spending a few weeks working through a text together via a weekly routine similar to the example one in Figure 6.5, we spend a week writing one of those essays. Each day in class is writing time that follows a brief mini lesson, perhaps looking at a mentor text together, or doing some instruction around an area of the IB rubric that students showed they need to work on, or focusing on a mechanical issue that will improve students' work. Students do some reader feedback for each other on one of those days, too.

### *Remind Students How the Weekly Routine Centers* Their *Work*

No matter the regular routine you design based on the needs of your particular curriculum, it's important to make clear to students exactly *why* the routine asks them to do the work they do. Offer periodic reminders where you show students the Three Step Meaning Making Process lined up with the specific tasks they're doing at each step. Project something like these the two examples shown in Figures 6.6 and 6.7 or ask students to tape them into their notebooks for class.

If students know the structures that underpin the routines they experience in our classroom, they will know *why* what they are doing each day and each week matters. They will know *how* it benefits them as readers, writers, and thinkers. This enables them to drive their work more effectively through the routines we design—an important way to share power with them.

**Our Meaning Making Process**

1) Start small (Reading):
    - Ongoing OTAs to capture what you think is important about any texts you read for class.
2) Seek Connections (Reading):
    - Rambling thoughts to build ideas across your OTAs.
    - Small-group and whole-class discussion about your ideas.
3) Take Action (Reading):
    - Decide what you want to write about inspired by the reading and the class discussion of it.
    - Write a rough draft.
4) Start Small (Writing):
    - Reflect on your rough writing in your writer's memo: if you were to keep working on the piece of writing, what would you focus on?
5) Seek Connections (Writing):
    - Find inspiration for how to improve your writing (based on what you said in your writer's memo) through mentor text study and reader feedback.
6) Take action (Writing):
    - Revise and polish your writing.

**Figure 6.6** Three Step Meaning Making Process Reminder for a Writing-Focused Class

**Our Meaning Making Process**

1) Start small:
    - Ongoing OTAs as you read our texts
2) Seek Connections:
    - Rambling thoughts to build ideas across your OTAs
    - Ongoing informal conversation about our texts with your table group
    - Weekly whole-class conversations
    - Periodic concept mapping invitations
3) Take action:
    - Articulate what you've figured out about the text in a formal essay.

**Figure 6.7** Three Step Meaning Making Process Reminder for a Reading-Focused Class

## Helping Students Feel Safe in the Classroom Space

Planning how your students will spend time in the classroom is one thing. Showing students how to *be* in the classroom space is another. What kinds of behaviors support or don't support the work? What are the daily routines? Where should they sit? And why there? How should they treat each other so that everyone in the room can be successful? How might their individual choices about the ways they conduct themselves in the room impact the other people in the community?

Over the years, I've come to realize again and again to assume nothing. Taking the time to show students what it looks like to be a member of the classroom community is well worth it in the end.

### *Classroom Procedures and Policies*

Taking a play out of *The First Days of School* (Wong & Wong, 2018) (which I regret not having read in year one of my teaching career), I am not one to flood my students with a huge list of class rules, policies, and procedures on the first day—or even in the first week—of school. I think about one or two things I can teach them each day, the things that are most critical for what we are doing on that day. After a few weeks, they've learned everything they need to know.

On the first day, for example, I emphasize what they should do when they come into class. I've got a seating chart posted for them, a roster posted next to the phone pockets to tell them which pocket to drop their phone into, and a task for them to start working on right away, quietly. As they come into the room, I greet them and keep repeating, "drop your phone off, find your seat on the seating chart, and start working on the task you'll see on the board." Once class starts and they're all working quietly, I might say something like, "Thank you for dropping off your phone, finding your seat on the seating chart, and getting started quietly on the task. That's how we'll start class every day. I appreciate you doing our start-of-class routine so awesomely on our first day together! Welcome to class! Keep working. I'll be with you in a few minutes." When they complete that initial task, we spend our time together on that very first day reading something, talking together about it, writing something, and reflecting on the work. From day one, students are doing the essential work they'll do in the class for the rest of the year.

We review all the other routines, policies, and procedures as they come up. First work to turn in? Great time to review how to turn in work, what the late work policy is, and what happens if they don't turn it in. First weekly check-in form to complete? Great time to review its purpose, how their responses inform instructional decisions for the next week, and why I ask them to do so much reflection. First silent reading session? Great time to review the expectations, how they should be using (and not using) the time, and what I'll be talking to them about when I crouch down next to their desk for a quick reading conference. First day to have their notebook in hand? That's when we review how we'll use the tool, where they can keep it in the room (if they wish), and how often I'll look at any work they do in their notebook. First small-group conversation? Review the basics of active listening and responding in ways that build conversation.

It may seem efficient to put all of these policies and procedures in one handy place, on one document or slide show, and review it all at once during one class rather than reviewing one or two items per day for the first several days of school. I find that a huge class policy/procedure dump like that communicates the wrong things to students. Reviewing all policies at once makes it difficult to have meaningful conversation about the purpose and intent of each individual one. Policies without clear purpose and intent can feel confusing or meaningless, and reviewing them can devour precious instructional minutes—especially when we talk about all the "right" ways to behave in the room and what will happen if students mess up.

For example, do you review your grading policy on day one, including how late and missing work will impact their grade and what will happen if they cheat or plagiarize? I get it—it feels important to get this out there up front. But think about what it says to kids: "The most important thing about this class is how I will grade you. And I am so certain that you will miss deadlines, not do work, and/or cheat that I have already made a detailed plan about how I'll handle it." That is not how I want to start the teaching/learning relationship with my students. A strict anti-cheating policy is far less effective than taking the time to talk about plagiarism—what it is, why students do it, why it hurts them as learners, and how to avoid it—at the moment where it's relevant. Like when they are working on their first pieces of writing. Especially with how the landscape is shifting with the arrival of artificial intelligence chatbots, our students need ongoing conversation—not detailed, punitive policies—to really understand how to drive the various resources widely available to them. Conversation can help students understand when chatbots can help them be better writers and when they get in the way of a writer's development.

That's a lot of words I've just written about only *one* policy you might have in your classroom. Each policy and procedure has reasons behind it, reasons that are important for students to know and think about. Those complexities get lost when we drone on about all of the class policies and procedures at once, in the first days of school, before students really even know us, the classroom, or each other.

### *Seating Charts*

The first day of school procedure I described above involves a seating chart. I'm a huge fan. With a seating chart, we show students that they have a spot reserved just for them in our classroom. For many students, it relieves them of the anxiety of coming into a classroom with no idea who else is in the class and having to choose a place to sit. For that reason, this is one area of the classroom I choose to drive. But not without student input.

I tell students that the first-day seating chart is temporary, that after a week and a half or so, they'll tell me who in the room they think might be positive for them to have in their learning pod that they'll sit with every day, and until then, they should learn what they can about every person in the room. To support this, we do some sort of whole-class get-to-know-you activities every day.

Though it takes me some time and energy to create seating charts, and I know many teachers decide they want to let their students make their own choices about where they sit, I find it critical for me to design the groups my students will sit with and the areas of the room where they will sit. Students are not privy to any individualized education programs (IEPs) and 504 plans that might dictate specific room locations for individual students. Also, they are not observing the class dynamics like I am over that first week and a half or so with an eye toward positive connections that seem to be forming, zones of distraction that might need some changing up, and students with shared interests who don't yet know that about each other.

But I am not aware of existing social dynamics between individuals in the class—so I ask (usually via a Google form): 1) Who in the room would be a positive force for you in a learning group? 2) Who in the room would NOT be a positive force for you? 3) Where in the room do you feel you would be most successful? I tell them with #2 that they don't have to give me any reasoning and that I will not share what they write there.

Taking into account my students' responses, my own observations, and any seating accommodations spelled out by individual IEPs and 504 plans, I construct learning pods for them to sit with each day. And then I watch carefully. Are the groups working? Do they need more small-group team-building time? Did I make a mistake anywhere that I need to correct? If the groups are cruising along well, I may leave them together for an extended time. The more they get to know each other, the more comfortable they will be sharing their thinking and their writing. It takes time to build those positive connections. But if I'm noticing some groups could use a shake up, or if I have any students tell me that something is not working so well in their group for them, I'll make some changes.

### *Community Building*

Once I've got my students sitting in learning groups I intend to last for some time—from a few weeks to a few months depending—we focus on community building. Students will feel safe to be who they are in a classroom where they feel connected to at least a few people in the room. And students who feel safe to be who they are will feel safe to take academic risks that lead to learning.

It doesn't take much time to help students forge connections with each other. Here are my students' favorite strategies lately:

**Minute to Win It**: A competition that lasts exactly one minute. Do an internet search on *minute to win it* and you'll find lots of possibilities, some more complicated than others. Here are a few I've used:

- Notebook paper ball contest: Ask students to get out their notebooks. They'll think you're going to make them write something, but no! They need one crumpled-up paper ball for their group and they will have one minute to see how long they can keep that paper ball in the air, bouncing it back and forth to each other with their notebooks. They count. If the paper ball hits the floor, they have to start over.
- Blind drawings: Write three random, easyish-to-draw items on the board. "Robot, chicken, shark," for example. Each student needs

a piece of scratch paper. Challenge students to put the paper on top of their heads and draw one of the three items, share their drawings with their groups, choose the best drawing, and post a photo of it to the class learning management system somewhere. All in one minute. Once all drawings are posted, scroll through them as a class, laugh, and decide on the best one.

- List as many _________ as you can: Each group needs a scribe. They will have one minute to generate as many items as they can together that the scribe will write down. It could be as many words as you can think of between two dictionary entries. Or it could be as many motifs as you can think of in the novel you're studying together. Make it connected to your current curriculum or something totally silly and separate. At one minute: "Pencils down! Count your items. Which group thinks they have the most?" Let the group read them off for the class to decide if they truly won it or not.

Perhaps the winners get a small prize—small plastic dinos (my students love these), custom haikus written by you, goofy stickers. Just make it something that will make them smile and forge positive associations with being in the classroom space.

I like that these one-minute competitions can be silly, they are infinitely customizable, they get students talking and laughing together, and they only take one minute. Surely you've got time for that!

**This or That**: Provide two options—cats or dogs for example—and tell students that if they prefer cats they go to one side of the room and dogs to the other. They have to choose one or the other. Once they get to the side of the room that lines up with their choice, they chat with the people around them about why they've chosen that side. After thirty seconds or so of chatter, pull the group together and invite a few responses from each side to see what students are thinking. A quick internet search will produce lists of this or that questions. But even better—invite them from your students. My students love using their own questions for this.

**Daily Questions**: Start class with about three minutes of informal small-group conversation: two minutes for talking in their groups and then one minute of sharing out with the whole class. It can be a great place for quick connections to the previous day's work, or to get students thinking about what's on deck for that day, or to deepen their thinking about a shared text, or to invite them to voice what *they* want to talk about.

More student-to-student conversation means more opportunity for them to forge connections with each other that will make them feel safe in the classroom space to take the risks necessary to learn.

## Co-Create Classroom Time and Space

Parker Palmer's take on the classroom space from *The Courage to Teach* is a vision that I aspire to:

> But for a space to be a space, it must be open as well as bounded—open to the many paths down which discovery may take us, to the surprises that always come with real learning. If boundaries remind us that our journey has a destination, openness reminds us that there are many ways to reach that end. Deeper still, the openness of a learning space reminds us that the destination we plotted at the outset of the journey may not be the one we will reach, that we must stay alert for clues to our true destination as we travel together.
>
> *(Palmer, 2017, 77)*

To actually achieve Palmer's vision, we need our students' help. As teachers, we establish the boundaries because we have to make sure the curriculum happens. We plan the course our students will drive as they practice the reading, writing, speaking, and thinking outlined by the learning goals for the classes we teach. But the boundaries must include flexibility. We can only do so much planning for what will happen in our classrooms. Once the thirty other humans in each class join us there, *their* needs, interests, and ideas about how things might play out complete our planning. That's the openness Palmer describes—to be ready for the "true destination as we travel together" with our students through our classroom space.

The community building I've already described in this chapter is an example of co-creating the classroom space. I've used This or That for years in the first week of school for whole-class community building, but my students have started asking for this more frequently. Now it's a weekly event on whole-class discussion days at students' request to help them warm up for talking with each other about class content. And the daily question strategy is something my students specifically asked for. When we were doing a mid-year reflection together on how things were going, they asked for more informal group conversation about class content. I reminded them that they sit in table groups and can literally talk to each other every day about what we're studying. But they wanted a few minutes of class time dedicated to it and an invitation from me to start talking. So that was how we started class on most days for the rest of the school year.

Our students can help design what happens in our classrooms. When we invite them to do so, we make room for their agency and show them that their ideas matter. It builds their confidence and cultivates their engagement and ownership—all critical to students being able to drive their own learning.

It's not just the day-to-day space of the classroom that students can co-create with us. Once students have been through several weeks of driving the course of learning you designed with the learning goals and the learning progressions based on those goals, invite them to closely examine the learning progressions and make suggestions for revisions. I have done this at the start of the second semester to reconnect students to the learning progressions ahead of creating their second semester plans for learning and growth.

I asked each new table group to look at the learning progression for one of the learning goals and present their recommendations for changes. They could suggest items to delete, or ways to reorder the progression, or ways to extend the learning for a particular learning goal. From the conversation we had around their brief, informal presentations, we established some new class routines (the aforementioned daily question), they voiced some additional supports they wanted from me (like a place to collect reading material relevant to the texts we're studying together in class), and they improved the learning progressions.

My students' revisions of the learning progressions were all still within the bounds of the curriculum. They created extensions on the learning, improvements on the sequencing, and enhancements to capture what they wanted to focus on. Their second semester plans for learning and growth were honed, specific, and meaningful. Their revisions to the learning progressions created a *better* guide as they set their own learning goals for the second half of the school year. But more importantly, the process invited conversation that strengthened their connections with each other and me. It showed them that there is space in our classroom for *their* ideas about how and what they want to learn. And it invited them to drive a really important piece of their experience in the classroom—the very curriculum itself.

Remember the driving course diagram from Chapter 1? What we're aiming for with our classroom space is stance 6, the one where we find ourselves on the edge, watching our students driving around in the classroom space we've designed. Every so often, we should invite students to join us at the edge to look over the course and help us think about how we can improve it together. From that vantage point, we can see places to add a few more directions, or a new road sign, or a traffic cone with something you want to emphasize for students. We can see when students might be ready for a bigger road to drive.

## The Goal Is Independence

It's whole-class discussion day for my sophomores. And the principal has just walked in to do a formal observation for my yearly evaluation. I've asked the table groups to find a panel they think the class should talk about from that week's section of Satrapi's (2004) *Persepolis*. As I'm making my way around the room to check in with each group, I notice a small waffle iron heating up at one table. And a small bowl of what appears to be waffle batter.

"What's happening?" I whisper to the three students sitting at the table.

"We're making waffles," they whisper back.

"How can you assure me that the waffle making won't disrupt today's discussion?"

"We'll be really quiet."

I pause, take a peek at the principal who is getting herself set up to take notes, and look back at the waffle chefs. I decide I want to see how this waffle thing will play out.

As I move the class out of small-group conversation and invite each group's representative/s to the seminar table, I notice there's now a bottle of maple syrup next to the waffle iron. As I listen carefully to the conversation developing at the seminar table, a sweet, waffly aroma wafts into the classroom space. But the whole-class conversation continues with no disruption.

Once the conversation wraps up, I address the class.

"I'm not sure if you all have noticed the waffle-making operation happening over here."

"We wondered if *you* noticed!"

"Of course I noticed." With a giggle, I turn to the waffle chefs. "How do you think making waffles impacted your ability to listen to the conversation today?"

They hold up their listening task sticky notes to show me they had listened well enough to fill three sticky notes each with their thinking about what their classmates said about *Persepolis*.

"Okay. Thank you! Now, thinking of our weekly routine, is there a day of the week that might be a better choice for making waffles?"

They look across the table at each other for a few beats of silence until one of them yells out, "Friday! During work time! Can we make waffles on Fridays!?"

"As long as you clean up after yourselves, and as long as you still get your work done, it doesn't matter to me."

For the rest of the school year, they made waffles every Friday. They shared them with the whole class. Everyone still got their work done. And when the bell rang at the end of class each Friday, the only evidence left was the waffle scent hanging in the air.

In nearly three decades of teaching, this was a first. Though it wasn't the important *academic* risk-taking that traditional grading prevents (see Chapter 5), I still took it as a positive sign that my students felt safe enough in the classroom space to risk making breakfast in class with no warning. A different version of me as a teacher might have shut things down at the first appearance of the waffle maker. (Especially on a day when the principal was there to evaluate me!) Instead, I saw it as an important community-building opportunity. My students were reaching out to co-create the classroom space. With some negotiation of ground rules together, we figured out a way to make waffles a beloved part of the weekly routine.

In a classroom anchored on student-driven instruction, we set up structures that enable students to explore on their own as readers, as writers, and as community members. As we negotiate and co-create with them what happens in the curricular and classroom space we've so carefully designed, they learn and practice key skills they'll use later to pursue who they want to be and what they want to achieve in their lives.

CHAPTER 7

# STUDENT-DRIVEN LEARNING MAKES *OUR* WORK MORE SUSTAINABLE

Up to this point, this book has been about crafting classrooms to put our students out front, classrooms that invite them to engage as authentically as possible in meaningful work that *they* drive.

But student-driven teaching isn't only better for our students.

*This* chapter is about *us*.

Teaching through the pandemic changed me as a teacher. During the 2020–1 school year, my campus and district crafted a schedule to account for the extra time teachers would need to figure out how to teach fully online at the start of the year with an anticipated shift to classrooms where we had some students on a screen via video and some sitting right there in the room with us. We had fewer classes to plan and fewer students in each term to manage, and we had Mondays to prepare for the week's instruction. It was the first time in my entire teaching career where I didn't feel like I had to work on the weekends to keep my classroom running.

My biggest hope for the following year was that we wouldn't just jump right back into the frenetic schedule our school days and weeks ran on pre-pandemic. I hoped we would take the time to really evaluate what we learned from the changes we made to make the pandemic teaching manageable.

But, as you can imagine, our schedule looks exactly the same as it did before the pandemic. Except now, I'm far less willing to take significant work home in order to keep my classroom running.

If I'm not sleeping enough, or if I'm not making time for yoga and hikes and walks, or if I'm not protecting time to love the people closest to me in my life, or if I'm not giving myself time to read books that I'm not teaching or to write more than lesson plans, I'm unhealthy as a human. Unhealthy humans cannot show up to their classrooms in a healthy way. My shift to Point-Less grading back in 2014 took some of the pressure off, but still, there are expectations around this job that seem impossible to meet without a significant time commitment beyond our contracted school day.

The system isn't going to make the necessary changes that will result in a more manageable work/life balance. So we have to make those changes ourselves. Designing a classroom based on student-driven learning is one powerful change to implement that makes the job more sustainable overall for us.

## Student-Driven Learning Saves Us Time Planning and Preparing for Class

As Chapter 6 explains, part of designing a classroom where students can drive their own work is establishing a regular routine that protects time for them to do that student-driven work. A predictable routine is important for students, but it also simplifies our planning. If you have a structure for what will happen generally in class on each day of the week, then when you sit down to plan, you've already got a framework to work with. You're not having to build each day's lesson plan from square one.

Chapter 5 reminds us of the importance of narrowing down our curricular expectations to a clear set of ten or so learning goals that can sit at the center of our classrooms. Students use that narrow list of goals to determine their own plans for learning and growth, and we can use that narrow list of goals to drive our instructional planning. It takes time to keep revisiting a complex list of curricular expectations; a narrowed list that captures the most important work can keep us focused when we plan, making that planning work faster.

The centerpiece in this book of a student-driven classroom is the Three Step Meaning Making Process. When we are teaching students how to make their *own* meaning via the reading strategies of Chapter 2, the writing strategies of Chapter 3, and talk strategies of Chapter 4, it absolves us of the responsibility of being the expert in the classroom, the holder of the answers, the one who knows all. Stepping out of that role so that our students can step into it saves us preparation time.

For example, no longer must we spend significant time studying the texts we invite our students to read so we can guide them to find what's most important. Instead, we are teaching *them* how to determine that importance. We still need to read the texts we are teaching, of course, but only to be ready to discuss them with students as simply another reader in the room rather than *the* expert. This reminds me of the first year I taught Allende's *The House of the Spirits* (2005) in Advanced Placement (AP) Literature. I read it for the first time on the same schedule as my students. We came to discover it together. My students were driving our conversations about the text, so it wasn't all on me to plan ahead of time what those conversations would cover. And I could pay attention to where they were struggling with the text based on their conversations and follow up with instruction targeted to support their learning.

In a student-driven classroom, some traditional classroom assessments get repurposed. For example, what you may have used in the past as a reading quiz or test to hold students accountable with a high-stakes grade for doing the reading can now be a tool for students to check their own comprehension of a text. As such, we don't have to do all the things necessary to protect the integrity of a high-stakes test. It's okay if students talk with each other over the answers. It's okay for you to use the same set of questions for all of your classes or from year to year. It's okay for students to check for themselves which answers they got right and wrong—you may never even need to look at it. It's okay to even use an artificial intelligence chatbot to write multiple choice questions for you! (If you do this, I recommend adding one final question for your students to answer: "what did the chatbot get wrong about the book when it wrote these questions?".) Writing high-stakes tests and quizzes can take significant prep time—time you can reclaim in a student-driven classroom.

Finally, Chapter 6 offered some ideas for co-creating with students. Students can carry some of the cognitive burden of making decisions about the classroom. We don't have to make all of the decisions alone. In fact, seeking student input can improve the classroom experience for all—sharing power with students engages them authentically, making their time in the classroom more meaningful, which decreases student behavior issues. Together with my students, we have figured out approaches to classroom work that I never would have seen on my own.

## Student-Driven Learning Saves Us Time Responding to Students' Work

Students need feedback on their work. It just doesn't have to all come from us. Chapter 4 describes the whole-class workshop approach outlined by Chavez in *The Anti-Racist Writing Workshop* (2021). Chavez's workshop protocol frees the teacher from preparation ahead of time. The student prepares for the workshop by thinking about the help they most need on the piece of writing. No prep work on the teacher's part. You read the work at the same time as the rest of the class does at the start of the workshop. No need to read it ahead of time. You give your feedback on the spot, as one voice in the workshop conversation. No need to write comments on the student's work. Obviously the one student whose work is the focus of the workshop will get extensive feedback. But all the students in the room benefit from the conversation, too. Ask them to look at their own writing and think about what they could change based on the whole-class workshop conversation.

Because student-driven grading avoids putting high-stakes grades on individual pieces of student work, many possibilities open up that aren't feasible with a traditional grading approach. Students can self- and peer-evaluate on evaluative rubrics when the rubric scores aren't grades that calculate into an ever-changing, high-stakes grade. Instead of tools for evaluative grading, these rubrics become tools to keep peer conversation about each other's work focused on the curricular goals the work targets. Evaluative rubrics can also guide student reflection on their own work. Both peer conversation and student self-reflection are opportunities for meaningful feedback that don't require the teacher's time.

Another approach to consider (that doesn't require you to spend hours evaluating and responding to student work) is to design tasks the class can do with students' finalized end-of-unit writing. For example, it might make sense for students to complete a significant writing task as a culminating assessment for a course. But the last thing I can manage at the end of the semester is a large stack of papers to grade.

Instead, what if the purpose of a culminating piece of writing was something more meaningful for the students? What if you came up with ways for students to work with each other's final pieces of writing? Rather than reading to grade their writing, you could read to decide which other student in class would be the ideal reader for each piece of writing. Students could read one classmate's essay and write a detailed letter of response to it, possibly guided by a checklist that addresses the curricular focus of the writing. That letter of response could be the ticket into a fishbowl-style conversation, wherein each student speaks of the piece of writing they read, and the students work together to talk out what the selection of papers they read together say collectively about whatever the focus of the writing task was. Through a series of maybe three fishbowl seminar conversations, each individual student's writing becomes the focus of class conversation for a few minutes. That plus the detailed letter of feedback from a peer adds up to far more feedback than you could give each student yourself.

These kinds of engaging tasks for students to do with each other's polished work frees you from having to read it in the ways that are most exhausting (at least for me). I just can't stare down a stack of thirty or sixty or ninety or more papers with a rubric and a quick turnaround time anymore. Plus, it's far more meaningful for students to prepare their work for something other than the teacher's red pen. Needing to have it ready for an important classroom community event is a much more meaningful reason to finish the work.

When we do have to evaluate work, not needing to have a high-stakes grade to put in the gradebook creates different ways to go about it. For example, my International Baccalaureate (IB) Literature students' drafts of the eventual external assessment really should get a score on the IB rubric, so students get a sense of how they're doing with the skills outlined on the rubric. They self-evaluate on the rubric—but getting my take as well is helpful. And it's important for me to go through their work with the rubric to assess how they're doing with the skills so I can figure out how to help them improve over time. As explained in Chapter 6, students draft one of these essays at the conclusion of our study with each major text. Because students won't be starting their *next* attempt at the same task until we finish a few weeks reading and discussing another text together, I can use those few weeks to read and rubric score their *first* attempt, with enough time to maybe read three or so per day, determine rubric scores for them, and make some notes for myself about what I want to teach students with the next essay to help them get better at the task. Three papers per day is something I can accomplish during my prep periods at school—no need to take the work home.

## Student-Driven Learning Saves Us Time on Data Management

Chapter 5 suggests that we shouldn't constantly evaluate students for a grade, that it gets in the way of the teacher-learner relationship, that students will be less likely to take the academic risks that lead to learning if they are worried those risks might negatively impact their grade. But the reality is that you likely need to have data in your gradebook—so quantify what makes the most sense to quantify: whether or not students are doing the work.

This shift is good for students because it gets them more focused on learning and less focused on point collecting for grades. But this shift helps *us*, too. Determining whether or not a task is complete (sometimes using a descriptive rubric as described in Chapter 5, sometimes just with a quick glance at the work) is a far easier task than evaluating it. We can assess for completion with less energy and time. We can still generate the volume of gradebook data our school communities might expect, but doing it is more sustainable.

As Chapter 5 explains as well, we can invite students to help us keep track of whether they've completed the work or not. It's a meaningful moment of reflection to have students look at a list of the tasks they should have completed over the past week and check off the ones they did—five tasks out of six done or all four out of four for a given week, for example. In this way, students generate a numerical data point you can quickly put in the gradebook.

It's definitely more sustainable to focus our gradebook data on completion. Completion data are easier to collect, and we can even enlist our students to help. But what about the pressure on us to ensure that our grades accurately reflect student achievement toward curriculum standards? We are just one piece in a larger assessment system that evaluates student achievement toward curriculum standards. There are required district and/or state testing and the AP and IB exams and assessments attached to those classes. Why do we need to constantly evaluate students, too? It's not good for our students, and it's not sustainable for us.

Another place students can help us with data management relates to conferences. Notes about the one-on-one conversations we have with students help us to make the best use of this powerful instructional strategy. But I've found the recording of conference data so onerous that at times it keeps me from actually doing them. We can turn over to students both the scheduling of conferences and the notetaking after each conversation. Start by determining how many weeks it would take you to get through a five-minute conversation with every student in the time you have available in class. (For me, it's four or so weeks, depending on the class.) Then, post an assignment in your learning management system titled something like, "Conference #1 with your teacher." Include a shared document with days/times for students to sign up for conferences (name, topic, day) and some instructions to guide students for preparing for each conference. When it's time in class for some conferences, open up the schedule to see who has signed up and start your conversations. At the conclusion of the conference, ask each student to return to the assignment to write a comment that captures what you talked about and what their next steps are with the work. If you keep using the same conference assignment—updating it for each round of conferences—then students will have a running list of their notes about their conversations with you. It's a rich data source for them to track their own growth and for you to see—in one place—the history of your conversations with each student. A data source that took *you* very little time to create.

IF YOU FIND YOURSELF THINKING...

This all might work for you but I have to drive things in my classroom because my students need more direction—yours are clearly more self-directed.

I have heard it all:

Sure, you can do that with your on-grade-level students, but it would never work with advanced students. They want an expert to tell them what they need to know. They like traditional grading.

Sure, you can do that with advanced students, but it would never work with other students. They need more direction and they need traditional grading to be motivated.

But ALL students will benefit from a classroom that puts them out in front, driving their own learning.

If they feel ownership over their work, they will be more engaged.

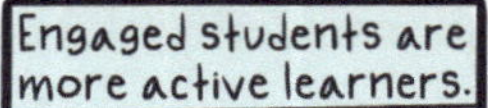

Engaged students are more active learners.

Active learners are more self-directed.

Self-directed learners know how to learn what they need for the rest of their lives.

We have to trust that our students truly WANT to drive their own learning and that we can teach them how.

IF YOU ALSO FIND YOURSELF THINKING...

My school/district/department expects something different. Until that changes, there's not much I can do.

Of course I cannot fully understand your teaching context or the challenges you're up against.

You are the expert on the needs of your students, your school, and your community and how those needs show up in your classroom.

I hope that stories from my classroom in this book and the glimpses of my students I provided have been an invitation for you to think about your own setting.

But, as Parker Palmer reminds us in The Courage to Teach, if there comes a time when the needs of the institution come into conflict with the deepest truths we hold about the experiences we hope for our students...

...we must find a way to follow those truths.

Only in the face of [opposition to the institution] has significant social change been achieved (170).

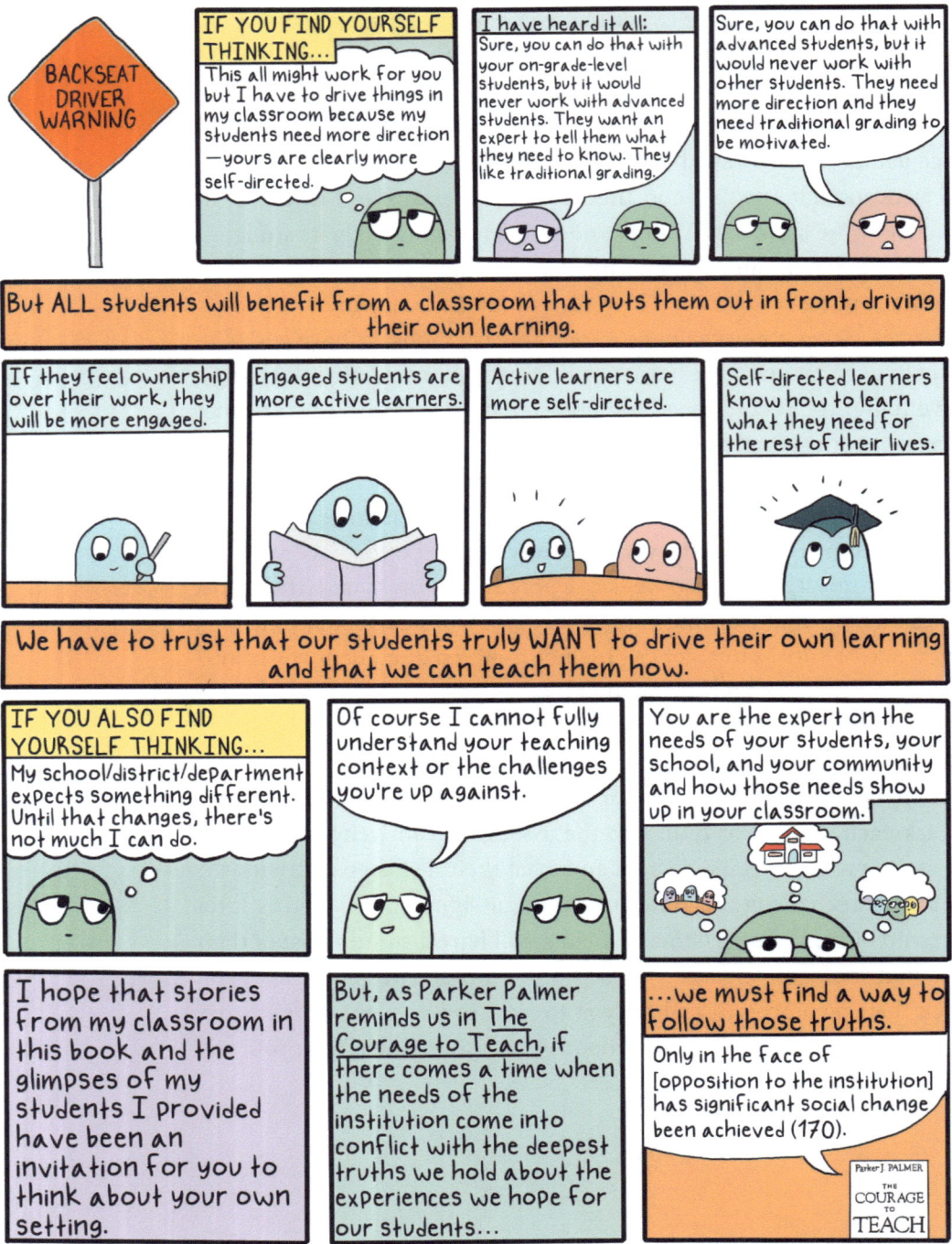

**Figure 7.1a** Backseat Driver Warning

Whatever change we can make in our classrooms matters for our students.

Maybe it's using OTAs and rambling thoughts alongside a prescribed reading program.
Original Thought annotation
I notice...
I think...

Maybe it's placing more emphasis on process and revision within a prescribed writing program.
Student
10:02 Today
I made this change because...

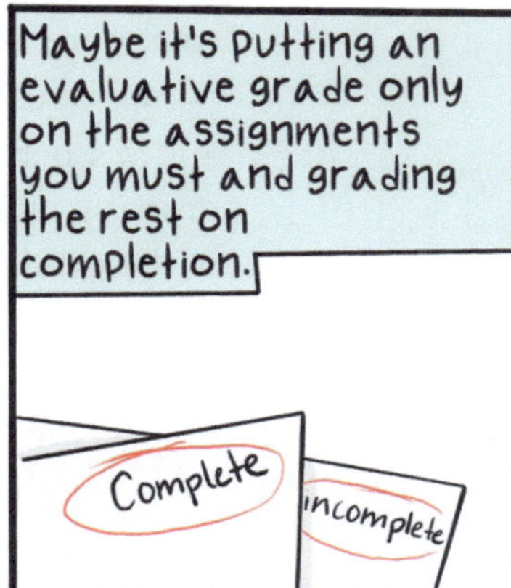
Maybe it's putting an evaluative grade only on the assignments you must and grading the rest on completion.
Complete
incomplete

Maybe it's finding like-minded colleagues to talk and plan together.

Maybe it's speaking up at a school board meeting to advocate for your students' ability to drive their own education.

And look closely at the standards that evaluate your teaching.

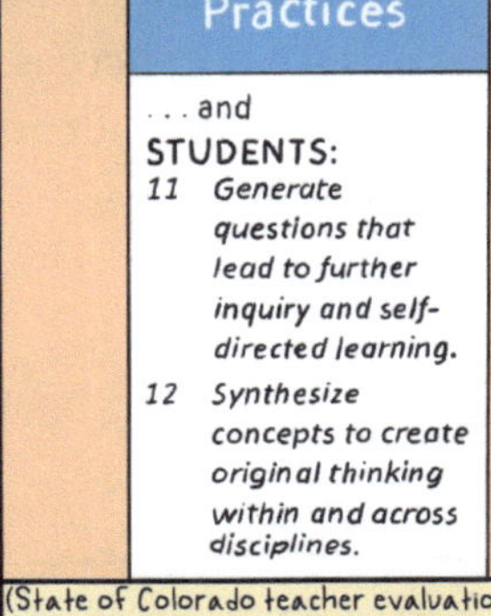
Exemplary Practices
. . . and
STUDENTS:
11 Generate questions that lead to further inquiry and self-directed learning.
12 Synthesize concepts to create original thinking within and across disciplines.
(State of Colorado teacher evaluation rubric)

Though it may seem your context expects something other than the student-driven vision of this book, that vision might be exactly how your institution defines best practice!

Figure 7.1b

## When Students Are Driving, They Do More While We Do Less

Students who are truly driving their own meaning making in our classrooms are stepping up to do *more* while we can step aside to do *less*. This is better for us because it means for a more manageable teaching experience, and it's better for our students because it means they are learning and growing more. So many of the solutions proposed to address the impacts of the pandemic on students' learning are too teacher-directed, too much based on constant evaluation, and too scripted. They strip students and teachers of their agency in the classroom.

But we won't always be there in our students' lives, telling them what to do and think in the time ahead and letting them know how well they are learning anything.

If we are serious about offering students classroom experiences that prepare them to meet the challenges of the rest of their lives, we have to show them how to drive through the complexity they'll encounter.

We have to show them that on their own, they know how to look at any text, no matter how complex, and start to discern meaning by simply noticing what they notice and building their ideas from there.

We have to show them that they can figure out any writing task on their own by studying mentor texts and leaning into the messy process of writing in order to figure out what they want to say.

We have to show them that they have the ability to express their ideas and listen to the ideas of others so they may use conversation to evolve their own thinking.

We have to show them that they have the power to set goals—large and small—for themselves, monitor their own progress, and reflect along the way to keep angling toward the success they hope to achieve.

We have to step aside so our students can truly drive, both in our classrooms and into the rest of their lives.

# Bibliography


Abdurraqib, H. n.d. *Published Work*. Hi. I'm Hanif. I write poems. I write Things About Music. I am probably eating french fries. Available online at https://www.abdurraqib.com/publications. Accessed 26 May 2024.

Acevedo, E. 2018. *The Poet X*. New York, NY: HarperCollins.

Allende, I. 2005. *The House of the Spirits* (M. Bogin, Trans.). New York, NY: Alfred A. Knopf.

Anderson, J. 2005. *Mechanically Inclined: Building Grammar, Usage, and Style into Writer's Workshop*. Portland, ME: Stenhouse Publishers.

Atwood, M. 1998. *Surfacing*. New York, NY: Knopf Doubleday Publishing Group.

Baca, J. S. 2001. *A Place to Stand: The Making of a Poet*. New York, NY: Grove Press.

Beers, G. K., and Probst, R. E. 2012. *Notice & Note: Strategies for Close Reading*. Portsmouth, NH: Heinemann.

Beers, G. K., and Probst, R. E. 2016. *Reading Nonfiction: Notice & Note Stances, Signposts, and Strategies*. Portsmouth, NH: Heinemann.

Blau, S. D. 2003. *The Literature Workshop: Teaching Texts and Their Readers*. New York, NY: Boynton/Cook Publ.

Bruner, J. 2002. *Making Stories: Law, Literature, Life*. New York, NY: Farrar, Straus, and Giroux.

Camus, A. 1989. *The Stranger* (M. Ward, Trans.). New York, NY: Knopf Doubleday Publishing Group.

Chavez, F. R. 2021. *The Anti-Racist Writing Workshop: How to Decolonize the Creative Classroom*. Chicago, IL: Haymarket Books.

Dersape, S. (Director). 2019. *Antigone* [Film; film]. Marc Daigle.

Ebarvia, T. 2024. *Get Free: Antibias Literacy Instruction for Stronger Readers, Writers, and Thinkers*. Thousand Oaks, CA: Corwin Press.

Edmundson, M. 2004. *Why Read?* New York, NY: Bloomsbury.

Elbow, P. 1998. *Writing with Power: Techniques for Mastering the Writing Process*. New York, NY: Oxford University Press.

Ellison, R. 1995. *Invisible Man*. New York, NY: Knopf Doubleday Publishing Group.

Espinoza, J. J. 2018. *"Things Haunt."* poets.org. Available online at https://poets.org/poem/things-haunt. Accessed February, 2023.

Faulkner, W. 1990. *As I Lay Dying*. New York, NY: Knopf Doubleday Publishing Group.

Filkins, S. "Socratic Seminars | Read Write Think." *ReadWriteThink*. Available online at https://www.readwritethink.org/professional-development/strategy-guides/socratic-seminars. Accessed 30 June 2023.

Fitzgerald, F. S. 1925. *The Great Gatsby*. New York, NY: Scribner.

Flash Fiction Online – Bold. Brief. Beautiful. Fiction in Fewer Words. Available online at https://www.flashfictiononline.com/. Accessed 23 February 2023.

Franzak, J. K. 2008. "On the Margins in a High-Performing High School: Policy and the Struggling Reader." *Research in the Teaching of English* 42 (4): 466–505. Available online at http://www.jstor.org/stable/40171812.

Gallagher, K. 2011. *Write Like this: Teaching Real-world Writing Through Modeling & Mentor Texts*. Portland, ME: Stenhouse Publishers.

Green, J., and Levithan, D. 2011. *Will Grayson, Will Grayson*. New York, NY: Speak.

Greene, M. 1995. *Releasing the Imagination: Essays on Education, the Arts, and Social Change*. San Francisco, CA: Josey-Bass, A Wiley Company.

Hamid, M. 2017. *Exit West: A Novel*. New York, NY: Riverhead Books.

Hammond, Z. 2015. *Culturally Responsive Teaching and The Brain: Promoting Authentic Engagement and Rigor Among Culturally and Linguistically Diverse Students*. Thousand Oaks, CA: SAGE Publications.

Hinton, S. E. 1967. *The Outsiders*. New York, NY: Viking Press.

Homer. 2018. *The Odyssey* (E. Wilson, Ed.; E. Wilson, Trans.). New York, NY: WW Norton.

Inoue, A. B. 2015. *Antiracist Writing Assessment Ecologies: Teaching and Assessing Writing for a Socially Just Future*. Fort Collins, CO: WAC Clearinghouse.

Inoue, A. B. 2020, Fall. "Grading Writing is a Racist Practice." *Statement* 53 (1): 1–13.

Jones, S. G. 2022. *My Heart Is a Chainsaw*. New York, NY: Gallery/Saga Press.

Kittle, P., and Gallagher, K. 2021. *4 Essential Studies: Beliefs and Practices to Reclaim Student Agency*. Portsmouth, NH: Heinemann.

Kohn, A. 2011. "The Case Against Grades (##)." *Alfie Kohn*. Available online at https://www.alfiekohn.org/article/case-grades/. Accessed 29 June 2023.

Kohn, A., Boggiano, A. K., and Pittman, T. S. 2022, September 21. *Why Feedback Often Doesn't Help*. Alfie Kohn. Available online at https://www.alfiekohn.org/article/feedback/. Accessed 7 July 2023.

Krakauer, J. 1997. *Into the Wild*. New York, NY: Knopf Doubleday Publishing Group.

*Learning progression*. n.d.. International Bureau of Education. Available online at https://www.ibe.unesco.org/en/glossary-curriculum-terminology/l/learning-progression. Accessed 11 July 2023.

Lyman, F. 1981. "The Responsive Classroom Discussion." In *Mainstreaming Digest*, ed A. S. Anderson. College Park, MD: University of Maryland College of Education.

Marchetti, A., and O'Dell, R. 2015. *Writing with Mentors: How to Reach Every Writer in the Room Using Current, Engaging Mentor Texts*. Portsmouth, NH: Heinemann.

Minor, C. 2019. *We Got This: Equity, Access, and the Quest to Be Who Our Students Need Us to Be*. Portsmouth, NH: Heinemann.

Nazario, S. 2007. *Enrique's Journey: The Story of a Boy's Dangerous Odyssey to Reunite with His Mother*. New York, NY: Random House Publishing Group.

Newkirk, T. 2014. *Minds Made for Stories: How We Really Read and Write Informational and Persuasive Texts*. Portsmouth, NH: Heinemann.

Newkirk, T. 2017. *Embarrassment: And the Emotional Underlife of Learning*. Portsmouth, NH: Heinemann.

Newkirk, T. 2021. *Writing Unbound: How Fiction Transforms Student Writers*. Portsmouth, NH: Heinemann.

Nilson, L. B. 2013. *Creating Self-regulated Learners: Strategies to Strengthen Students' Self-awareness and Learning Skills*. Sterling, VA: Stylus Publishing.

Nussbaum, M. C. 1995. *Poetic Justice: The Literary Imagination and Public Life*. Boston, MA: Beacon Press.

O'Connor, F. 1971. *The Complete Stories*. New York, NY: Farrar, Straus and Giroux.

Owocki, G., and Goodman, Y. M. 2002. *Kidwatching: Documenting Children's Literacy Development.* Westport, CT: Greenwood Publishing Group, Incorporated.

Palmer, P. J. 2017. *The Courage to Teach: Exploring the Inner Landscape of a Teacher's Life.* San Francisco, CA: Wiley.

Pan, E. X.R. 2018. *The Astonishing Color of After.* New York, NY: Little, Brown Books for Young Readers.

Petrus, J. 2020. *The Stars and the Blackness Between Them.* Penguin Young Readers Group.

Prather, L. 2022. *The Confidence to Write: A Guide for Overcoming Fear and Developing Identity as a Writer.* Portsmouth, NH: Heinemann.

Pryle, M. 2018. *Reading with Presence: Crafting Mindful, Evidence-based Reading Responses.* Portsmouth, NH: Heinemann.

Rex, L. A., and McEachen, D. 1999, August. "If Anything is Odd, Inappropriate, Confusing, or Boring, It's Probably Important": The Emergence of Inclusive Academic Literacy through English Classroom Discussion Practices. *Research in the Teaching of English* 34 (1).

Roberts, K. 2018. *A Novel Approach: Whole-class Novels, Student-centered Teaching, and Choice.* Portsmouth, NH: Heinemann.

Rosenblatt, L. 1938/1995. *Literature as Exploration.* New York, NY: The Modern Language Association of America.

Salesses, M. 2021. *Craft in the Real World: Rethinking Fiction Writing and Workshopping.* New York, NY: Catapult.

Satrapi, M. 2004. *Persepolis: The Story of a Childhood* (M. Satrapi, Trans.). New York, NY: Knopf Doubleday Publishing Group.

Schulten, K. 2023, January 19. Respond to a Story in The Times via Our One-Pager Challenge. *The New York Times.* https://www.nytimes.com/2022/12/14/learning/respond-to-a-story-in-the-times-via-our-one-pager-challenge.html.

Schulz, K. 2014. "On Being Wrong." *TED*. Available online at https://www.ted.com/talks/kathryn_schulz_on_being_wrong?language=en. Accessed 29 June 2023.

Sophocles. 1962. *Antigone*. Translated by Michael Townsend, New York, NY: Harper and Row.

Stommel, J. 2020. "How to Ungrade." In *Ungrading: Why Rating Students Undermines Learning (and what to Do Instead)*, ed. S. D. Blum, 25–41. Morgantown, WV: West Virginia University Press.

Sumara, D. J. 2002. *Why Reading Literature in School still Matters: Imagination, Interpretation, Insight*. Mahweh, NJ: Lawrence Erlbaum Associates.

"Text Rendering Experience." 2017. National School Reform Faculty. Available online at https://www.nsrfharmony.org/wp-content/uploads/2017/10/text_rendering_0.pdf. Accessed 4 February 2024.

Thompson, M. E. 2018. "We're Killing the Love of Reading, but Here's an Easy Fix – Unlimited Teacher." *Unlimited Teacher*. Available online at https://www.unlimitedteacher.com/blog/were-killing-the-love-of-reading-but-heres-an-easy-fix. Accessed 29 June 2023.

Ward, J. 2012. *Salvage the Bones*. New York, NY: Bloomsbury USA.

Witherall, C. 1991. "The Self in Narrative: A Journey into Paradox." In *Stories Lives Tell: Narrative and Dialogue in Education*, ed. Witherall, C. and Noddings, N. New York, NY: Teachers College Press.

Wong, H. K., and Wong, R. T. 2018. *The First Days of School: How to Be an Effective Teacher*. Mountain View, CA: Harry K. Wong Publications.

Zerwin, S. M. 2020. *Point-Less: An English Teacher's Guide to More Meaningful Grading*. Portsmouth, NH: Heinemann.

# Index


accountability for work 100
agency, cultivating 11–12
artificial intelligence 141
assessment 85–6, 141; of conversation 81–2; of reading 33, 36–7; of writing 63–4; *see also* grading
assessment data sources 106–7

backseat driver warning 15, 22, 44, 50, 80, 95, 123, 146–7
book clubs 67–9

centering students 4–8
classroom talk 73–4
classrooms: co-creating time and space 135–7; community building 133–5; independence in 137–9; policies and procedures 130–2; routines 119–29; as safe spaces 130–5; seating charts 132–3
co-creating classroom time and space 135–7
community building 6, 133–5
concept maps 27–9
conversation 32, 67–9, 141; grading/not grading 81–2; independence 82–3; modeling writing conversations 75–6; one-on-one conversations 145; teaching students to talk with each other 71–81; Three Step Meaning Making Process 69–70, 77–9, 81
craft moves to study mentor texts 54–5
cultivating student agency 11–12

daily questions 134
data management 144–7
dependent learners 86
descriptive rubrics 102–5
designing classrooms *see* classrooms
driving metaphor 5–7

engagement 19
evaluating their own work 99–100
evaluative rubrics 104

feedback 55–8, 142–4
final grade letter/story, writing 112–14
finalizing writing 58–63
finding mentor texts 51–3

goal setting 87–8; strategies for ongoing reflection 97–9; *see also* learning goals
goals: independence 38–40, 64–6, 82–3, 114–16, 137–9; learning progressions 88–91; *see also* learning goals
grade description checklist 111
gradebooks: data management 144–7; what to put in score boxes 101–5
grading 33, 36–7, 85–6, 142; accountability for work 100; conversation 81–2; descriptive rubrics 102–5; final grade letter/story 112–14; guidelines for final grade selection 109–12; helping students see how fully and completely they are doing the work 101; helping students see their progress 107–9; independence 114–16; inviting students to help track their work 105–6; Point-Less approach 86;

rambling thoughts 102; students' self-evaluations 99–100; Three Step Meaning Making Process 114; what to put in score boxes 101–5; writing 63–4; *see also* assessment
groups, small-group shared work 32
guidelines for final grade selection 109–12

Harkness Table conversations 71–2
helping students: see how fully and completely they are doing the work 101; to track their work 105–6

independence 38–40; in classrooms 137–9; in conversation 82–3; in grading 114–16; in writing 64–6

just-right readers for feedback on writing 55–6

kidwatching 8

language use 105
learning behaviors 91–2
learning goals 8–10, 140; articulating learning behaviors 91–2; helping students see their progress 107–9; learning progressions 88–91; making plans for their own learning journeys 93–6; setting goals 87–8; *see also* goals
learning journeys, inviting students to make plans for 93–6
learning pods 132–3
learning progressions 86, 88–91
listening tasks 72

magic questions, writing 45–7
meaning making 3, 118; how to invite students to drive as readers 16–19; Three Step Meaning Making Process 9–10, 18–19; *see also* Three Step Meaning Making Process
mentor texts 51–5, 123
Minute to Win It 133–4
modeling: conversations 75–6; writing process with students 43–5, 48

not grading: conversation 81–2; reading 36–7; writing 63–4; *see also* grading

one-on-one conversations 145
original thought annotations (OTAs) 20–3, 118; learning goals 97–9

peer feedback 55–6
phantom policy 2–3
phantom teachers 3–4
planning for classes 140–2
Point-Less approach 86
policies in classrooms 130–2
polishing writing 60–3
preparing for classes 140–2
pre-teaching 16
procedures in classrooms 130–2
proofreading 59–60

rambling thoughts 24–7; grading 102
reading 16–19; independence in 38–40; inviting students to drive as readers 13–16; seeking connections 24–32; start small 20–3; taking action 33
reading-focused classes, routines in the classroom 121, 126–8
reflecting on day-to-day classroom, conversation 79–81
reflection, strategies for ongoing reflection 97–9
responding to students' work 142–4
revision tasks, writing 47–9
routines in the classroom 119–29
rubrics 102–5

safety in classrooms 130–5
seating charts 132–3
seeking connections: concept maps 27–9; conversation 32; rambling thoughts 24–7; small-group shared work 32; two-page spreads 30–2, 34; writing 49–58
self-evaluation on learning progressions 95
setting goals 87–8; strategies for ongoing reflection 97–9; *see also* learning goals
shared texts, teaching students to talk with each other to determine meaning from shared text 71–4

small-group shared work 32
Socratic Seminars 71–2
stepping aside to center students 4–8
strategies: for learning 8–10; for ongoing reflection 97–9
student agency, cultivating 11–12
student-centered discussions 71
student-driven learning: data management 144–7; planning for classes 140–2; responding to students' work 142–4; students doing more, while teachers do less 148
studying mentor texts 53–5

taking action: meaning making 33; on writing 58–63
thinking: rambling thoughts 24–7; seek connections 24–32
"Think-Pair-Share" method 69
This or That 134
Three Step Meaning Making Process 8–10, 140–1; grading 114
Three Step Meaning Making Process, conversation 69–70, 77–9, 81
Three Step Meaning Making Process, reading 9–10, 18–19; reading-focused classes 129; seek connections 24–32; start small 20–3; taking action 33
Three Step Meaning Making Process, writing 42–4; seeking connections 49–58; start small 45–9; taking action 58–63; writing-focused classes 129
two-page spreads 30–2, 34

white language supremacy 105
whole-class conversations 71–3
whole-class workshopping, a single piece of writing 77–9
workshopping, whole-class workshopping a single piece of writing 77–9
writer's memos 46
writing 41–4; cleaning up mechanics 59–60; feedback 55–8; final grade letter/story 112–14; grading/not grading 63–4; independence in 64–6; magic questions 45–7; mentor texts 51–5; modeling writing process with students 44–5, 48; polishing 60–3; revision tasks 47–9; seeking connections 49–58; start small 45–9; taking action 58–63; teaching students to talk with each other about their writing 74–9; Three Step Meaning Making Process 42–4; whole-class workshopping 77–9
writing-focused classes, routines in the classroom 121–6